MY FAMILY HISTORY

Results of research carried out by Brian Duncan

Volume 1
THE DUNCANS

Edited in April 2017

MY FAMILY HISTORY
Results of research carried out by Brian Duncan

Volume 1
THE DUNCANS

©2017 Brian Duncan
ISBN: 978-0-9915032-2-3

CONTENTS

Ancestors of Richard Houston Roan Duncan

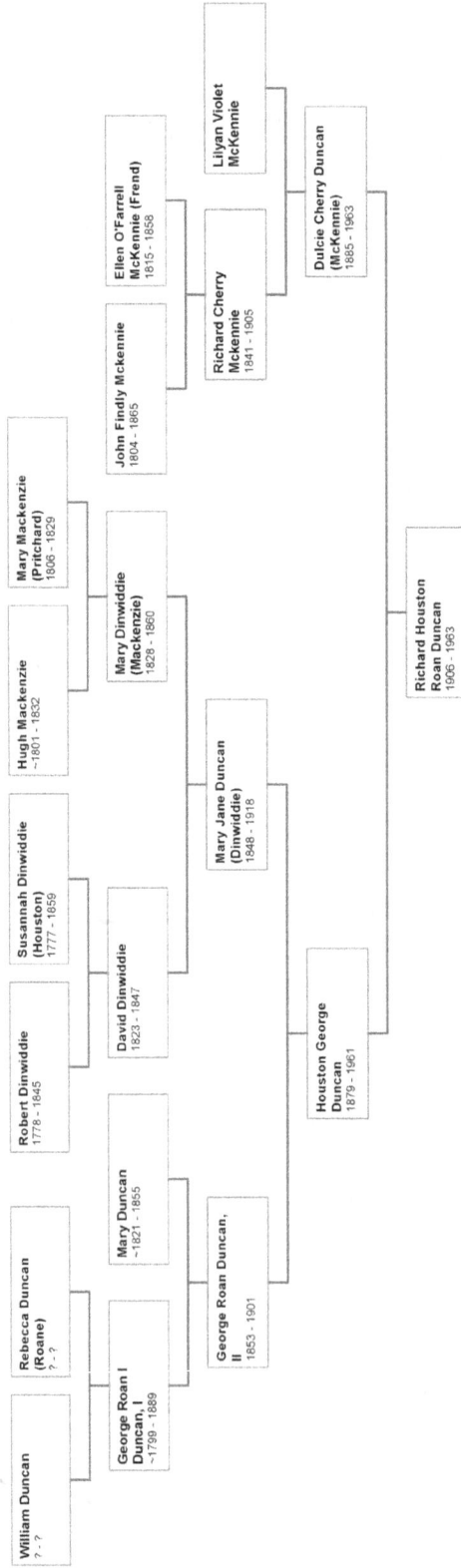

William Duncan
? - ?

Rebecca Duncan (Roane)
? - ?

George Roan I Duncan, I
~1799 - 1889

Mary Duncan
~1821 - 1855

Robert Dinwiddie
1778 - 1845

Susannah Dinwiddie (Houston)
1777 - 1859

David Dinwiddie
1823 - 1847

George Roan Duncan, II
1853 - 1901

Hugh Mackenzie
~1801 - 1852

Mary Mackenzie (Pritchard)
1806 - 1829

Mary Dinwiddie (Mackenzie)
1828 - 1860

Mary Jane Duncan (Dinwiddie)
1848 - 1918

Houston George Duncan
1879 - 1961

John Findly McKennie
1804 - 1865

Ellen O'Farrell McKennie (Frend)
1815 - 1858

Richard Cherry Mckennie
1841 - 1905

Lilyan Violet McKennie

Dulcie Cherry Duncan (McKennie)
1885 - 1963

Richard Houston Roan Duncan
1906 - 1963

INTRODUCTION

Foreword

I started researching my family history in 1975 and stopped about thirty years later. It's time to publish the information, intended only for family members. It's not an easy to read narrative – more a research document. I hope that someone will take over the role of family genealogist and will pick up the threads.

I also hope there are enough crumbs to interest you. Certainly there are gaps, such as my paternal grandmother's mother, whose family name remains unknown despite all my efforts to trace it.

I have ended the 'tree' with myself and siblings, deliberately not proceeding to our marriages and children, all of which you know.

Most of my research was done during short visits to the UK, when I was able to visit the British Library in London, and the Public Records Office in Kew, where the staff were extremely helpful. In the last third of the research period I found the Internet valuable, especially the Rootsweb groups.

I was fortunate to contact several relatives, some of whom I met, notably Ken Edmondson and his father Bill, from the Frend family, now living in Tennessee; also Denise Taylor, a descendant of Robert DUNCAN.

Layout

I have divided the publication into a series of volumes, one for each main branch of the family. Broadly, each book will cover the ancestors of a great-grandparent (see chart). However, we know nothing about one great-grandparent's ancestors, although this will be compensated by voluminous knowledge of the Farrington branch, ancestors of my mother.

Probable future volumes will be:

Volume 2: The Dinwiddies

Volume 3: The McKennie and Frends

Volume 4: The Brackens and Hirsts

Volume 5: The Farringtons

Volume 6: The Macleods

To make the text easier to digest I have taken some of the detail about more distant relatives into a series of Appendixes.

Formatting

Most of the text format follows standard genealogy practice, with each generation indented. However, I have introduced a few personal touches. The names of 'blood' relatives are underlined; they are in bold type for ancestors.

I introduced supercripts to designate relationship to me and my siblings. For example a second cousin is shown as ^{2}, a first cousin once removed as $^{1/2}$ and a great-great-aunt as ^{GGA}.

There are numerous footnotes, intended for anyone wishing to trace a source. Some refer to names of contacts, whose details may not longer be valid; indeed some of them may no longer be living! I am astounded by, and grateful for, MS Words ability to keep the footnotes in sequences throught my re-ordering of the text.

Relationships

There are many cousins in the document. A first cousin shares the same pair of grandparents. Thus Sue Bracken is my first cousin (unusually, my only one) because we share a pair of grandparents. Likewises, Caroline is a first cousin to Hector and Martin, and to Alex and Nicky, for the same reason.

Caroline is a first cousin to Angus, Duncan, Eleanor, Tucker, George, Florence, Oliver and Ella, but they are a generation apart, so they are first cousins once removed. You'll see, when the relevant volume appears, that William Wilberforce is my first cousin, but many times removed!

Second cousins share the same great-grandparents. So Jack and Sam are second cousins of Angus, Duncan, Eleanor, Tucker, George, Florence, Oliver and Ella. They don't share the same grandparents, but they do share a pair of great-grandparents, specifically my parents.

Acknowledgments

I'm deeply indebted to Phil and Roy for preserving a large collection of documents throughout their travels, and for giving me access to them. Also to Caroline, and latterly Tess, for encouragement and tolerance. Tess said that I was spending more time on my dead relatives than my living ones! That hasn't been true in the last ten years, when I have barely touched the documents. Several family members have been in contact with me, as indicated in the footnotes, and I'm most grateful for their contributions.

I've had much help from the staff at the India Office Collections in the British Library, and fellow members of the Families in British India Society. Names and information about other contacts are in the footnotes, but some of these are probably out of date.

I'm grateful to Doug Heatherly of Lighthouse for designing the cover, and for patiently helping me prepare the text for printing.

CHAPTER 1: THE EARLY DUNCANS

The first of our Duncans that I've been able to find, so far, is **William DUNCAN**, who married **Rebecca ROANE** in 1793. I have no information about the birth or death of William, but we know that Rebecca died in 1833, because a letter[1] from her son Robert (1866/67) says: *"...since our mother's death in 1833."*

A possible ancestor is William DUNCAN of Maughereydruman, in the parish of Donaghcavy, whose will was probated in 1716. The Duncans were probably Protestant settlers who came from Scotland in the 17th or 18th Century, and settled in and around Co. Limerick and King's County (Co. Offaly). Unfortunately, because so many Irish genealogical records were destroyed by fire, it will be very difficult to search for the ancestors of William and Rebecca, without going to Ireland. It seems probable that the Duncans originally came from Scotland, perhaps in the deliberate process of colonisation by Protestants. Also, William Duncan's son, George Roan Duncan I, told his son-in-law David Dinwiddie that his forebears 'hailed from the Land O' Cakes'.

I have virtually no information about the ROANE family, except some details sent by Brian Roane, about an ancestor who went to India from Galway in 1825. He may have been a relative of Rebecca ROANE, and one can speculate about a possible connection with George Roan Duncan 1's career (see below), but this connection has not been made yet.

Valuable information about the Duncans in Ireland comes from two letters written by Robert DUNCAN [2GGU] to his brother (my 2nd great-grandfather) **George Roan DUNCAN I** in 1866-67. These letters were preserved by my grandfather, and then by my sister Philippa and her husband Roy (the Ingram Archive!), and are transcribed in Appendix A. Other valuable information came from an autobiography and letters written by **David DINWIDDIE**, my 2nd great-grandfather, in 1865-1883 (see the forthcoming book about THE DINWIDDIES). His daughter, **Mary Jane DINWIDDIE** married **George Roan DUNCAN II** – they were my great-grandparents.

Most of the information I have collected myself has been about the Duncans in India, and has come from the Oriental and India Office Collections (OIOC) at the British Library in London (see preface). I have 'discovered' several hitherto unknown great-uncles and great-aunts, as well as cousins of varying degrees.

My grandparents named their farm in Malawi 'Rath Drum'. The only connection I've found with a Rath Drum/ Rathdrum in Ireland is the town in Co.Wicklow, where Louisa HALPIN grew up (see the end of this chapter). However, Cindy Wood[2] told me that there is a place of that name in Co. Offaly, in Balycommon Civil Parish, which lies on the border of Co. Offaly and Co. Westmeath

---

[1] See Appendix A.
[2] <cwood91262@aol.com> ; cellphone # 574-993-0443; office # 269-445-0257.

WILLIAM DUNCAN (bef.1775[3]-aft.1799), my 3rd great-grandfather, married **Rebecca ROANE** (bef.1780[4]-1833), my 3rd great-grandmother, in the parish church of Birr (Parsonstown), Co. Offaly, on 7 April 1793.

I wrote to the Rector of the church in 1985, and he replied quoting the exact entry:

> *'Mr William Duncan & Miss Rebecca Roane, both of this Parish of Birr, were married by Lycence this 7th day of April 1793 by me A.G/H. Downs junr. curate of Birr. Their marriage was solemnised between us* (signatures) *in the presence of* (three signatures impossible to decipher with accuracy)'.

In August 2005 I indulged in a rare piece of paid research through Eneclann[5], who sent me the following transcription:

> *'Mr William Duncan & Miss Rebecca Roane both of the Parish of Birr were married by licence this 7th day of April 1793 by me, A.G/H. Downs junr curate of Birr. This marriage was solemnized Between us W. Duncan, Rebecca Duncan. In the Presence of _ D. Kavanagh. A. McNamee.Thos.Palmer.'*

Note that for Birr Parish: baptisms (1760-1870); marriages (1760-1844); and burials (1786-1855) are on microfilm in the National Archives of Ireland (NAI).

Also: Protestants in some parishes of Co. Offaly are listed in *The Irish Ancestor* (1973), which can be seen in the SOG. Also: the 1821 Census data is in the NAI – one of the few that survived the 1922 fire.

A correspondent[6] thinks that it was probably Rebecca's family that came from Birr or Co. Offaly, because there is no recurrence of the Duncan surname in Offaly in the Griffith Valuations that would suggest that they had a long residence there.

A Lydia ROANE married George ELY on 18 July 1780[7], who might have been a sister or aunt of **Rebecca ROANE**. Her relationship to Rebecca ROANE is not proven. However, 'Lydia' was a family name. Furthermore, Robert DUNCAN, in his letter dated 13 March 1867 (Appendix A), writes: *"I and my poor wife feel very much for being situated as we are and only for the late Richard ELY we would now be in prosperous circumstances as he was the sole cause of our being deprived of our farm at Ballaghmore to secure it for himself which God did not let him enjoy long but I forgive him all the serious injury he did me."* Is it possible that this Richard ELY was the brother or son of the George ELY, who married Lydia ROANE in 1780?

I received recently some information from Patricia Roane Straube (straube@earthlink.net), who lives in San Francisco, and is descended from a ROANE family that lived in Birr, King's County (now Co. Offaly) and may well have been related to 'our' Rebecca Roane. Patricia Straube's ROANEs came over to the USA from Ireland in the 1830s. The name suggests a 'French connection'. Also, it seems that the name 'ROAN', which became a second name for many male Duncans, was a masculine version of ROANE. Cindy Wood says that Roan(e) has two separate origins: one is a variant of Rowan, from the tree. The other is from the French town Rouen, suggesting Huguenot origins.

---

[3] IGI has abt.1768 'of Killaloe Diocese', but no source quoted.
[4] IGI has abt. 1772 'of Killaloe Diocese'.
[5] Eneclann, Unit 1, Trinity Enterprise Centre, Pearse Street, Dublin 2, Ireland (+353-1-6710338; info@eneclann.ie; www.eneclann.ie.
[6] Cindy Wood
[7] IGI.

Birr (formerly Parsonstown) is on the River Birr, about 18 miles SW of Tullamore, and 60 miles WSW of Dublin, in Co. Offaly. The town has a long and interesting history. It had a flourishing distillery trade[8], and it is interesting that Robert Duncan, one of William's sons, worked in the trade (see below). Is it possible that William Duncan worked for a distillery firm?

It is also possible that William DUNCAN was a farmer, since his son Robert (who might have been the eldest son) owned a farm (see below). A William DUNCAN is listed in the Index of Prorogative Wills of Ireland as a merchant in Dublin in 1800. Another William DUNCAN was a farmer at Knockashangan (will probated in 1829, see Irish Wills).

Note that a William, John and James DUNCAN moved from Virginia to Dublin in 1774; they were originally from Strathblane in Scotland[9].

William and Rebecca DUNCAN had the following children, but unfortunately we do not know the order of their birth. According to the conventional naming patterns, the eldest male and female would have been named after grandparents, and the second children after the parents. Yet we have John, Robert, Thomas, and George, though not necessarily in that order, but no William - he might have died in infancy. The daughter Rebecca was no doubt named in honour of her mother. Does that mean that Lydia was a grandmother's name? Cindy Wood thinks that George Roan Duncan might have been the eldest son because he inherited the Roscrea property (see letter: Appendix A). However, I think it is more likely that Robert was the eldest and that George was left the Roscrea property by his mother.

1. Robert DUNCAN [2GGU] (aft.1793- aft.1866) had a house and farm at Ballaghmore, but lost them (he claimed) due to action by someone called Richard ELY (see letter dated 6 July 1866, or 1867, in Appendix A):

   "I have been treated very badly by Richard ELY who was the means of depriving me of my farm and house at Ballaghmore, he being anxious to secure the whole place to himself."

   There are several Ballaghmores in Ireland, and two Ballaghmore Castles! The most likely is the one in Co. Laois, in the Civil Parish of Kyle, Poor Law Union of Roscrea. Ballaghmore is not listed in Samuel Lewis' 'A Topographical Dictionary of Ireland (1837). My judgment was confirmed by Cindy Wood, who found Richard Ely in Kyle civil parish, Ballaghmore Upper and Lower, Queen's Co. (Co. Laois). There was also a Thomas Ely in the townlands.

   A Robert Duncan is recorded in the Roscrea civil parish, Co. Offaly, which borders on Lyle civil parish, Co. Laois[10]; he was in the townland of Drumakeenan, leasing a house from someone named Thomas Bergin, the estate agent for someone named Joseph Dwyer.

   On 13 March 1867, Robert wrote[11] from No.3 Westland Street, Limerick, to his brother **George Roan DUNCAN I** (then in India). Robert was working for Messrs.(?) Fitt and Sons, Newgate Brewery, Limerick. I have been told that *"...the Fitt family was into all sorts of things in Limerick City, solicitors, pawn shops, you name it. I doubt very much if anything as mundane as employment records survive..."[12].*

---

[8] DI, 1837.
[9] <apduncan@hotmail.com> (9.12.01).
[10] Primary Griffiths Valuation.
[11] See transcription of letter in Appendix A.
[12] pers.comm..: Cindy Wood (Jan.2003).

There is an indication in Robert's letters that his wife's name was Anne or Ann (probably WOODLOCK):

'*...am joined by Anne and Thomasina...*'[13], '*My nephew Thomas Woodlock*'.[14]

Note that a widow, Ann DUNCAN (aged 70, and therefore born about 1811) was an inmate at Leeds Union Infirmary, Beckett Street, Leeds, at the time of the 1881 Census. Could this have been Ann/Anne DUNCAN (née Woodlock), having gone to her son George after her husband Robert Duncan died?

Further information about the descendants of Robert Duncan is in Appendix H.

2. <u>John DUNCAN</u> [2GGU] (aft.1793-bef.1866). According to a letter written by his brother Robert in 1866/67: "*Our brother John is also dead. He went to America several years ago and died there.*" What did he mean by 'several years ago'. 'Several' usually means 2-3, or at least less than 10, but in this case we have to think of about 1840-1864.

There were 29 John Duncans, born in Ireland, recorded in the 1850 US Federal Census. I have therefore concentrated my search among those born in the period between 1793 (when the parents were married) and 1820:

a. **John DUNCAN** (b.c.1794) was recorded[15] in E. Fallowfield, Crawford County, PA, aged 55, a farmer, with Sam (?), his wife (?), 38, and children: **William** (18), David (16), **John** (14), Henry (12), Mary (6), Joseph (4), and James (2). The wife and children were all born in PA.

b. **John DUNCAN** (b.c.1797) was recorded[16] in Brown Twp., Miami County, OH, with his wife, who he married (1819) Deborah KNOOP, in Canada, and moved to Miami County, Ohio in 1822. Their children were: **William** (22), Nancy (20), **Thomas** P. (18), and Martha J. (15). There was another, separate family headed by David (36), a blacksmith, with children: Martha J. (4), **Lydia** A. (2), and Margaret (19).

c. **John DUNCAN** (b.c.1798) was recorded[17] in the 3rd Ward of New York, NY, a merchant, living without wife or children.

d. **John DUNCAN** (b.1799) was recorded[18] in the 5th Ward of New York, NY, a cooper, living with his wife Margaret (40).

e. **John DUNCAN**, 'of Donegal 1804' came to the USA and settled in Somerset County, Pennsylvania, and was married to Susan GRIFITH (GRIFFITH?) a Quaker[19]. He was recorded with Susan (44) and children named: **George** (22), **Rebecca** (20), **William** (11), and Sarah J. (8). The names 'William', 'George', and Rebecca' are family names, and clues to a possible relationship. They do not appear in Pennsylvania in the 1860 Census. The boys

---

[13] Letter No.2 from Robert Duncan to George Roan Duncan (13 March 1867).
[14] Letter No 1 from Robert Duncan to George Roan Duncan I (6 July 1866/7).
[15] M432_771 (p.421).
[16] M432_771 (p.427).
[17] M432_535 (p.325).
[18] M432_537 (p.259).
[19] message from Lenora McMillan (3.7.99) in Duncan Family Genealogy Forum (http://www.genforum.com/duncan/)

would have been old enough to fight in the Civil War, but there are so many George and William Duncans that the search would be daunting.

3. Rebecca DUNCAN [2GGA] (aft.1793-aft.1866) . Her brother Robert wrote (1866/67): *"Rebecca is also in very good circumstances and has been receiving the rent of the Roscrea property (which is yours) since our mother's death in 1833."*

We do not know whether Rebecca married [a Rebecca DUNCAN married William JOHNSON (or JOHNSTON) in Drumcree, Co. Armagh in 1828. I have no proof this is the same person, but the date seems to fit].

Rebecca lived in Kilkee, Ireland, in the mid-1860s, probably with her widowed sister Lydia[20]: *'They have not given me the least assistance, although they are very comfortable at Kilkee, a beautiful sea bathing place'*[21].

4. Thomas DUNCAN [2GGU] (aft.1793-c.1863). According to a letter written by his brother Robert in 1866/67: *"I have just received your kind letter of the 7th May last, from the widow of our late Dear Brother Thomas. The poor fellow died at Clonmel three years ago. He left his Daughter and Wife well provided for."* There are several Clonmels in Ireland, but the most likely is the one in Co. Tipperary. There are no Duncans in the Griffith Primary Valuations for Co. Tipperary[22].

Thomas married a person unknown, and had a daughter:

> a. daughter DUNCAN [1/3] (c.1830-aft.1866) mentioned in Robert Duncan's letter (see above).

Note that Clonmel's 1821 Census data survives in the NAI. Clonmel house and occupiers are in Parliamentary Papers, Reports from Committees (Vol.II (2), 1837), also registered voters.

The 1851 Griffith's Valuation has an index of householders in Co. Tipperary.

5. **George Roan DUNCAN I** (c.1799-1889), my great-great-grandfather, about whom more in Chapter 2.

6. Lydia DUNCAN [2GGA] (aft.1793-aft.1866). She is mentioned in the letters of her bother Robert, written in 1866/67 (Appendix A).

Lydia married Francis KENNEDY (bef.1815-c.1865) on 18 May 1835, in St. Mary's Church, Limerick[23]. He was a Captain in the Army or Navy[24], and was recorded as 'Francis

---

[20] see Appendix A. Transcript of two letters from Robert Duncan.
[21] Letter No.2 from Robert Duncan to George Roan Duncan I (13 March 1867).
[22] Pers.comm.: Cindy Wood (Jan.2003).
[23] IGI.

M. KENNEDY' in the IGI listing of the marriage of his son William (see below). He seems to have leased several properties in Co. Clare, in Kilfearagh and Kilfiddane Civil Parishes[25].

Robert DUNCAN wrote (1866/67): *"Captain Kennedy died a short time since and left Lydia very comfortable."* St Mary's is a Church of Ireland church, although Francis is a Catholic name, so it is unlikely that Lydia married a Catholic. We can guess from the names of his children (below) that Francis' father was named Francis, and that his mother was named Eleanor.

Lydia and Francis had (at least) three children[26]:

a. Francis Duncan KENNEDY [1/4] (c.1839- ?) was baptised on 7 May 1839 at St Michael's Church, Limerick. Note the first name honours the father, and the second name the mother's family.

Note that a 'France' KENNEDY (b.1838) married Honora McELLIGOT in 1863 in Limerick. We need to find out whether this was 'our' Francis.

b. Eleanor Rebecca KENNEDY [1/4] (c.1840- ?) was baptised on 1 June 1840 at St Michael's Church, Limerick. I suspect that Francis' mother was named Eleanor. 'Rebecca' is the maternal grandmother's name.

c. William Hugh Harris KENNEDY [1/4] (c.1841- ?) was baptised on 31 December 1841 at St Michael's Church, Limerick. 'William' is the maternal grandfather's name. Hugh might be the paternal grandfather's name.

William married, on 9 April 1866 at Rathdrum, Co. Wicklow, Ireland, Louisa HALPIN. She was born at Rathdrum in 1845, the daughter of James Halpin.

William and Louisa had at least three children:

i) female KENNEDY [2/3] (1868- ?) was born on 18 June 1868 at 1044, Ashford, Wick, Ireland, recorded in the civil registration of Wicklow[27].

ii) Francis Frederick KENNEDY [2/3] (1869- ?) was born in Co.Wicklow[28], possibly in the same place as his brother Robert (below).

iii) Robert Charles Halpin KENNEDY [2/3] (1873- ?) was born on 31 March 1873 at Ashford, Wick, Ireland[29].

Note that St Michael's is a Church of Ireland church, and its records include: baptisms (1803-1871); marriages (1803-1845); and burials (1803-1889) – on microfilm at NAI.

---

[24] Letter No.1 from Robert Duncan to George Roan Duncan I
[25] Cindy Wood – from the Primary Valuation.
[26] IGI: Batch # C700571, film 0883696.
[27] FHL Film 101166 (1868-1869) from Cara Links (cracker@hotkey.net.au) (6 August 2004).
[28] Cindy Wood (pers.comm).
[29] FHL Film 255877 (1873-1874) from Cara Links (cracker@hotkey.net.au) (6 August 2004).

Lydia probably lived as a widow with her sister Rebecca in Kilkee: "*I very seldom see ......* *sisters. They are too pr*[oud to] *visit me as I suppose they*[think we] *are too poor. They have not given me the least assistance, although they are very comfortable at Kilkee, a beautiful sea bathing place*"[30].

Note:

DUNCAN, Rebecca	Marr.	Sept. 1884 Qr.	Middlesborough (9d, 693)
DUNCAN, Rebecca	aged 26, b. Stockton, Middlesborough (1901 Census)		
DUNCAN, Rebecca	aged 40, b. Ireland, living in Southampton, a domestic nurse (1901)		
WOODGATE, George Roan	Death	Dec. 1842 Qr.	Shoreditch (2, 314)
WOODGATE, George Roan	Birth	Sep. 1871 Qr.	Lewisham (1d, 774)
WOODGATE, George Roan	Marr.	Mar. 1886 Qr.	Greenwich (1d, 968)

---

[30] See Appendix A: Transcript of two letters from Robert Duncan.

CHAPTER 2: GEORGE ROAN DUNCAN I

GEORGE ROAN DUNCAN I (c.1799-1889), my 2nd great-grandfather, married three times and fathered at least eleven children – we may never know how many! He was reputed to have lived to be 99, although I discovered that he actually died at the age of about 90-94. Even so, a grand age for the 19th Century. He sounds as if he was quite a character. Though quite small in stature, he must have had a courageous personality, and determination to rise through the ranks of the Honourable East India Company's army, to become a Warrant Officer (Conductor) and then an honorary officer. In his own words he *"raised himself from the position of a poor and friendless soldier to that of Captain in her Majesty's Indian Army"* (see below).

We are fortunate to know as much as we do about him, partly through his testimonials in support of his petition for an army commission, and partly from references about him in the letters of his son-in-law David DINWIDDIE (1818-1883).

There is a painted portrait (below), supposed to be of G. R. DUNCAN I, now with my nephew Hector INGRAM, in Wilmington, NC, USA. Thanks to my daughter Caroline for taking the photo.

George Roan DUNCAN I (c.1799-1889)

Although not clear in this image, the portrait shows Lieutenant's pips on the old soldier's epaulettes. Note the white solar topi on his right. It ought to be possible to verify the subject of the painting through expert identification of his uniform.

I have no record of his birth, which almost certainly took place in Ireland. However, the approximate year can be imputed from three sources:

a. 1798/1799 from his military record[31] which states:

> *'Ship "Herefordshire", 30 January 1817* [presumably the date of departure], *George DUNCAN, Madras, Infantry, age 18, 5 ft.6/12 in., long visage, brown hair, hazel eyes, fresh compn., born in Parish of Birr, King's County, Ireland, enlisted by Captain Grange in Dublin, attested 6 December 1816 for unlimited service as labourer'.*

b. 1796/1797 from the record of his 3rd marriage (age 61 on 5 March 1858);

c. 1799/1800 from his brother's letter (*'nearly 17 when you joined the army'*)[32].

d. circa 1795, based on his death record in L/AG/34/14A/271, which says that he was 94 when he died in 1889.

I think the first estimate (1798/1799) is the most likely, and that he exaggerated his age in later life.

He may have been born in Birr, a town now called Parsonstown in the present Co. Offaly (formerly King's County), on the border with Co. Tipperary. His death record[33] states that he was born in 'Parson's Town/Birr, Ireland'. I wrote to the Rector of Birr in 1981, and he replied (11 March 1981):

> *"Dear Mr Duncan,*
>
> *Re: George Roan Duncan*
>
> *Thank you for your letter of 1st March. I have checked carefully through the records of Birr Parish. There is no record of the baptism of George from 1795 to 1802. In fact there are no Duncan baptisms at all in that period. As a matter of interest I did come across the Marriage record of William Duncan and Rebecca Roane on 7th April 1793.*
>
> *If they are in fact the parents of George, I can only assume that although married here, they must have left the district before any family arrived. No addresses are given in the Marriage entry, only that they are both 'of this Parish', that is the Parish of Birr.*
>
> *Sorry if this information does little to throw light on your research.*
>
> *Yours sincerely,*
>
> *(Rev. Canon) D. L. Keegan"*

---

[31] OIOC (L/MIL/9/42 & L/MIL/11/101).

[32] See Appendix

[33] OIOC (L/AG/34/14A/271).

It was this letter that enabled me to trace the marriage of William Duncan (see Chapter 1). It would seem, therefore, that George, and perhaps his siblings as well, were baptised in another parish. Roscrea is a prime candidate. The Roscrea baptism records for 1784-1878 are in the National Archives of Ireland in Dublin (Microfilm MFCI3, M5222)[34].

His date of attestation was 6 December 1816, and date of arrival in India was 26 June 1817[35]. His period of service when he attested was 'unlimited'[36]. The journal[37] (log) of the *Herefordshire* shows that she sailed from Gravesend on 12 February 1817, and landed her passengers at Madras on 26 June 1817. Major General Dyce was on board, and the ship's commander was William Money.

The East Indiaman 'Herefordshire' in 1813

This oil painting by W. J. Huggins shows the *Herefordshire* off Margate, Kent, in 1813. As is common with pictures painted to the order of the owner, the ship is shown in three positions (broadside, from the bow and from the stern). She was built in Bombay, carried a crew of 130 men and was armed with 36 guns. Like other East Indiamen, the *Herefordshire* was privately owned but was chartered by the Honourable East India Company, to whose specification she had been built.

---

[34] Gresham, J. 'Tracing Your Irish Ancestors'.

[35] OIOC (L/MIL/11/101).

[36] OIOC (L/MIL/9/41).

[37] OIOC (L/MAR/B/49).

According to a letter[38] from David Dinwiddie, written in 1874: *"...the hardy old gentleman was with Generals Doveton and Hislop's columns during the Maratha War 55 or 56 years gone by."* David Dinwiddie also wrote[39] in 1875: *"The old man is about 76 years of age* [i.e. confirmation of birth in 1799] *and over 59 years in India. He is still able for work and can gallop his saddle horse 24 miles before breakfast every morning of the week for a pinch. He was soldiering during the Pindarah War with the Maharrata Chiefs in 1818 and 1819 when I was only one year old!!!"*, and *"... he was born in Ireland, his forefathers having 'hailed he believes from the Land o' Cakes'* [Scotland]. "

George DUNCAN summarised his career in a 'Memorial' to the Secretary of State for India, in 1863:

'To the Right Honorable the Secretary of State for India.

The humble and most respectful memorial of George Duncan, Lieutenant Veteran Establishment - Deputy Assistant Company[40] of Ordinance[41] - Madras Army.

Humbly sheweth:

That your memorialist having faithfully zealously and to the best of his Ability served in your Indian Army for Forty seven years, the greater portion of which in the Ordinance Department of it, and having always during that time performed his duties most of them of a most responsible and even confidential nature, to the entire satisfaction of every Officer under whom he has been placed - now ventures most humbly and most respectfully to pray that you, Right Honorable Sirs, will be pleased to confer on him the rank of Captain, which has already been conferred on several of your memorialist's comrades.

II. Your memorialist begs leave most respectfully to submit for your consideration, Right Honorable Sirs, the following brief sketch of his career in the Indian Army, which, together with the character he bears amongst those of his superiors to whom he is known, form the ground whereon he presumes to make the present application.

III. He enlisted as a Private of Infantry in the late Honorable East India Company's Service in 1816, and on arrival in India joined the Madras European Regiment (Fusiliers)[42] and served in that distinguished Corps during the whole of the Maharatta Wars of 1817/18/19, in which Regiment he continued to serve till 1832 (the latter six years in the arduous and important situation of Regimental Serjeant Major, when he was promoted to the Warrant Officer Grade of Sub Conductor and subsequently to full Conductor in the Ordinance Department, in which your memorialist served for twenty eight years, during which period he has made several difficult and fatiguing Marches in charge of Convoys of Military Stores, all to the satisfaction of his superiors.

IV. On the decease of the Rajah of Nagpore, and the annexation of his Country to Her Majesty's Dominions, the Commissioner of the Province was pleased to appoint your memorialist to the responsible position of Duputy Assistant Commissary of Ordnance - a position involving entire charge of the late Ruler's Park of Artillery, Munitions of War, Arsenals, and very extensive Military Stores and Equipment, can conscientiously assert that he has thoroughly realized what was expected

---

[38] David Dinwiddie to General Blake, 4 Sept.1874.

[39] DD letter (January 1875).

[40] Probably a mistake in transcription - should be 'Commissary'.

[41] Probably a mistake in transcription - should be 'Ordnance'.

[42] The regiment became 1st Madras (European) Fusiliers in 1843

of him - During the said Mutiny of 1857, your memorialist, made himself useful in many instances; on the night of the 13th June, when Seetabuldee was threatened with an Attack, he was the first European at the Grand Arsenal, and with the sanction of Major Bell, then Commissary of Ordnance, lost no time in getting into position four 9 Pdr. Guns, had them manned and loaded, prepared to meet any emergency - Your memorialist further undertook the duty to Patrol the road from the Arsenal to the City of Nagpore during which tour of duty he arrested a native Cavalry soldier, coming with all speed from the City, and disarmed him by taking his Pistol from him, delivering the same to the Adjutant of the Corps (Lieutenant Morris) who was much pleased at this Act of daring - A few days after this, matters at the City of Nagpore appeared in a very critical position, and the Commissioner of the Province was very desirous that a large quantity of Gun Powder which was lodged in a Magazine of the late Ruler's, distant from the Cantonment 5 miles, should be destroyed; also that a number of Arms, Accoutrements, and a large quantity of Gun and small Arm Ammunition, should be removed into the Grand Arsenal, which duty your Memorialist was deputed to perform and which was carried out much to the Commissioner's satisfaction.

V. Your Memorialist has on various occasions been placed in Charge of Details of the Horse Field Battery attached to the Nagpore Irregular Force; and has also held Charge of, and made arrangements for, Horses purchased by the Commissioner of the Province, for the Service of the Government in the North West Provinces, in all of which duties he has given satisfaction.

VI. Your Memorialist further ventures to hope that the annexed Copies of Testimonials, from the Officers whom he has served under, may have some influence in bettering his present position, and that in conjunction with his long and faithful service they may justify him in offering himself as a candidate for further promotion to the rank of Captain, a boon which has already been conferred on many of his Comrades, as mentioned in the 1st Paragraphs of his Memorial.

VII. Finally, your Memorialist desires to plead the cause of a large and young family; your Memorialist cannot expect to be many more years spared to them; Carefulness has enabled him to make some provision for them, but nothing that your Memorialist can bequeath to them would be so valuable as the proud boast if their Father having by faithful service, and exemplary conduct, raised himself from the position of a poor and friendless soldier to that of Captain in her Majesty's Indian Army, should your Memorialist be so fortunate as to obtain the promotion herein solicited, and your Memorialist as in duty bound will ever pray.

(Sgd.) George Duncan, Lieutenant Veteran Establishment and Deputy Asst. Commissary of Ordnance, Madras Army. Seetabuldee, 11th February 1863.

Old Fort and cannon at Sitabuldi, Nagpur

Cannon at Sitabuldi Fort

The main sources of information about his career are the printed '*Testimonials: obtained by Lieut. George Roan Duncan, Deputy Assistant Commissary of Ordnance, during the period passed in the service of Government, from the Year 1816.*'. The document was dated 11 February 1863, and each testimonial carries a date, and the range is 2 March 1829 to 8 February 1861. An original handwritten version, bearing George Duncan's signature (see below), is in the possession of my sister. The version in the Appendix was printed at some time later.

These testimonials give some clues to his military service. One of the testimonials is from Capt. William MORRIS of the Nagpur Irregular Cavalry, dated 27 September 1860, and states: *"I have the greatest pleasure in thus bearing my testimony to the wonderful energy and marked coolness displayed by Lieutenant DUNCAN on the night of 13 June 1857. This gallant old officer on hearing of the outbreak at Nagpur, at once proceeded to the Arsenal, and there made every preparation to meet the expected attack of the insurgents. During the night he also patrolled the various roads leading to the city, and single-handed, gallantly attacked and disarmed a rebel Sowar. His conduct on this, as I believe it has on other occasions, drew forth the highest praise from those who knew how bravely he had done his duty on that eventful night."*

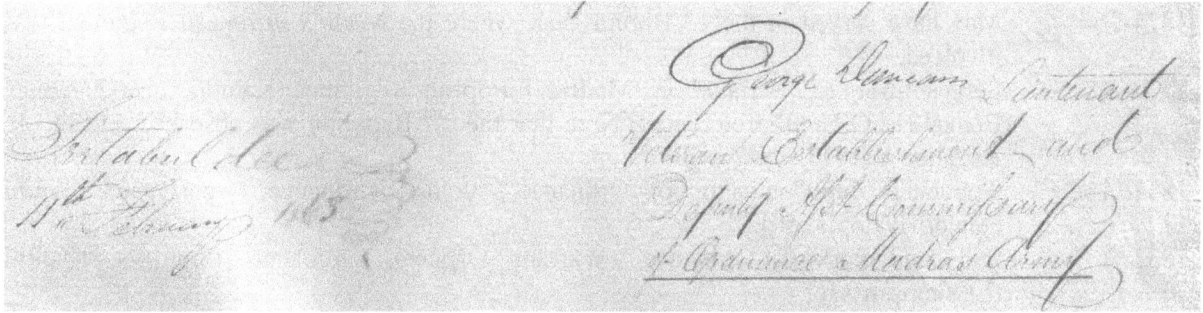

George Roan DUNCAN's signature in 1863

Chronological record of George Roan DUNCAN I's life:

ca.1798/1799   Born (probably) in the parish of Birr (Parsonstown), King's County (Co. Offaly), Ireland.

1816, Dec.6   Attested 'for unlimited service as a labourer' (in the army of the Honourable East India Company) in Dublin.

1817, Jan. 30   Embarked (probably in Dublin) for India on the *'Herefordshire'*.

1817, June 26   Arrived at Madras, India, on *'Herefordshire'*.

1817-18   David Dinwiddie wrote in a letter that GRD *'was soldiering during the Pindarah War with the Maharata Chiefs in 1818 and 1819'*. However, the 3rd Mahratta War (also known as the Pindari Campaign) was in 1817-18, and in his own Memorial (dated 11.2.1863) George Duncan states: *"..Maharatta Wars of 1817/1819"*. The Pindaris were irregular bandit cavalry which flourished in central India in the late 18th and early 19th centuries, sometimes serving the Mahratta states. G.R.Duncan would have been in this campaign because David Dinwiddie wrote (in 1874) *'the hardy old gentleman was with Generals Doveton and Hislop's columns during the Mahratta War 55 or 56 years gone by'*. Brigadier General Doveton commanded the 2nd Division of the Army of the Deccan which assaulted Nagpur on 16 December 1817, after the town had been captured by Mahrattas under Bhonsla, whose 21,000 strong army was routed. Sir Thomas Hislop's 1st and 3rd Divisions of the Army of the Deccan (5,500 men) engaged the Mahratta army (35,000 strong) on 23 December 1817 at Mahidpore. The Madras Europeans were among the few Europeans under Hislop's command. This battle virtually ended the 3rd Mahratta War[43].

1817-1822   Married Petronella, an Indian or Eurasian (marriage record not found).

1823, June 17   His daughter Ellen baptised at Masulipatam.

1825   Sergeant-Major, 2nd Battalion, Madras European Regiment (under Major Gibson) (Col. Miller's ref.: in App.A). He was then aged about 26. The former Madras European Regiment was divided in 1824 (Col. Duke's ref.). Note that between 1779 and 1839, the regiment was known as The Madras Regiment. From 1839 it was The Madras (European) Regiment.

---

[43] HAYTHORNTHWAITE, Philip, 'The Colonial Wars Source Book', quoted in http://members.ozemail.com.au/~clday/pindari.htm

1824-26	May have served in the 1st Burma War, where the Madras European Regiment was involved.
1829	Sergeant-Major, 2nd Battalion, Madras European Regiment, Kamthi (near Nagpur), Bengal (Lt.O'Neill's reference). Note that the 2nd Battalion was absorbed into the 1st Battalion in 1830.
1832, Apr. 13	Appointed Sub-Conductor of Ordnance[44]. Joined Ordnance Department, Kamthi (Major Hyslop's ref.).
1835	Sub-Conductor of Ordnance (Warrant Officer), Ordnance Dept. at Kamthi (Lt.Simpson's ref.).
1840	Married for the 2nd time in Kamthi, as a widower, to a widow, Mary PASLEY (née LEECH).
1841	Daughter Eliza baptised at Kamthi.
1844	Conductor of Ordnance, Nagpur Subsidiary Force, Kamthi (Major Hyslop's ref.). His son, William George Duncan born in Kamthi.
1846, June 8	Daughter Mary Laura baptised at Kamthi.
1847, June 25	Witnessed baptism of grandchild Charlotte CAMPION, at Sitabuldi, Nagpur.
1850, June 16	Witnessed baptism of daughter Lydia Rebecca at Kamthi, near Nagpur.
1854	Conductor of the Arsenal at Sitabuldi (Major Spence's ref.).
1855	Deputy Assistant (the Acting Assistant) Commissary of Ordnance, with the rank of Conductor, Nagpur Irregular Force, Kamptee and Sitabuldi (Mr Ramsay's ref.). Daughter Mary Faith baptised at Sitabuldi.
1857	In Nagpur during mutiny activities on 13 June (Capt. Morris's ref.).
1858	The HEIC Army was amalgamated into the British Army after the Indian Mutiny. Promoted to Lieutenant in the Madras Veteran Establishment (aged about 61) (Major Elliot's ref.), and soliciting for the rank of Captain (Col. Boileau's ref.).
1858, Mar.5	Third marriage, to Alice WILSON, at Sitabuldi, Nagpur, described as 'Commissary of Ordnance'.
1859, July 20	Witnessed marriage of daughter Eliza to Theodore CRAWLEY, at Sitabuldi, Nagpur.
1861	In Sitabuldi, described as 'Lieutenant' in baptismal record of his son, John Gillespie Duncan.
1863, Feb.11	Submitted petition to promoted to Captain.
1868, Feb.25	Witnessed marriage of his son William to Thomasina DUNCAN, at Sitabuldi, Nagpur.
1869, July 14	Witnessed baptism of granddaughter Anna Mary DUNCAN, Sitabuldi, Nagpur.
1872, Mar.18	Witnessed baptism of grandson G.W.R. DUNCAN, Sitabuldi, Nagpur.
1875	David Dinwiddie, whose daughter married the son of G. R. Duncan I, described him as 'Captain Duncan'.
1875, July 20	Witnessed marriage of daughter Mary Faith, at Sitabuldi, Nagpur.
1885, Jan.7	Witnessed marriage of son Henry Lauder, at Sitabuldi, Nagpur.
1888	The Nagpur and Berar Times (22 December 1888) describes him as 'Lieutenant George R. Duncan, of the Madras Veteran Establishment' and 'now very close upon his centenary' though he was in fact only about 90 at the time.
1889, 16 Jan.	George Roan DUNCAN died at Nagpur, Bengal, aged about 90-91.

---

[44] OIOC (L/MIL/11/101).

The Madras European Regiment was in the 1st Infantry Brigade (Lt. Col. Robert Scot) of the Army of the Deccan (Lt. Gen. Sir Thomas Hislop), according to Wilson, W.J. Lt. Col. "History of the Madras Army (1746-1826)" (1888, vol.4. OIR 355.31). It appears that the Regiment did not take part in the relief of Nagpur, but were in the Battle of Mahidpore, with nine officers and 314 men.

The 1st Madras European Regiment were sent to Pegu, Burma, in October 1825 (206 'rank and file'), and formed part of the 1st Division (Brig.Gen. Cotton) in the advance on Prome. On 26 November they were involved in the Capture of Pegu. However, in George Duncan's memorial (end of chapter) there is a quote: *"Our acquaintance commenced above thirty two years ago (in 1825) when you were Serjeant Major of the then 2nd Madras European Regiment under Major (the late Major General Gibson) who I know entertained the highest possible opinion of you"*. Thus it would seem that George Duncan did not go to Burma in 1825, otherwise he would have mentioned it in his testimonial.

On 1 February 1830 the 1st and 2nd Regiments were formed into a single Regiment, known as the Madras European Regiment. The 2nd (battalion?) MER became the 1st MER on 15 October 1839.

Esmond FOSTER (according to Chris WHEELER's notes[45]), wrote that George DUNCAN I: *"...fought through the Mutiny of 1857. Received official commendation for slaying mutineers with his own sword before Delhi. Later, he commanded Fort Nagpur and subsequently lived at Camperdown House, built on a ridge near the fort and named after one of the great naval victories which was won by one of his ancestors - Adam DUNCAN."* The above records show that this account is not accurate, as often happens in family histories. Furthermore, there is no known connection between our DUNCANS and the celebrated Admiral!

David Dinwiddie wrote[46]: *"Last month my Wife's eldest son George Delahoyde ventured down from the hills, Dalhousie, and got spliced to the youngest daughter of* <u>*Captain*</u> *Duncan, so our families are now doubly joined"*. But David Dinwiddie also wrote: *"We always address the good old man as Capt. Duncan, although he is only Lieutenant in the Invalided Establishment, he draws his full pay, and is on receipt of a handsome salary as a member of the conveyance or Bazaar Committee!"*[47]

A copy of Nagpur and Berar Times, Sat. 22 December 1888[48] states: *"We observed our much esteemed and venerated Lieutenant George R. DUNCAN, of the Madras Veteran Establishment, among those assembled to do honour to his Royal Highness; and he was personally presented by the Brigadier General to the Duke of Connaught, who seemed to be much pleased to meet the old gentleman, now very close upon his centenary. It must have fired once more the gallant old soldier's heart when he mentioned to H.R.H with pride that he thought himself to be, in fact, was almost certain he was, the oldest soldier in India, if not in the whole of the British Army, having effectively served in four successive reigns - those of George III, George IV, William IV and her present Most Gracious Majesty Victoria - 'God bless her', as the veteran soldier exclaimed. And we understand that the Prince very graciously asked Lieut. DUNCAN for two copies of his photograph, one to retain himself and the other to send to his august mother the Queen Empress"*. I don't understand the phrase 'now very close upon his centenary', as he would have been about 90 in 1888. The occasion was only weeks before the old man's death.

---

[45] See the chapter: THE GILMORE-FOSTER Family.

[46] DD letter to General Blake, 30.8.1875.

[47] DD letter to Margaret (Jan.1873).

[48] Ex Ingram Archive, now in my possession.

George Roan DUNCAN I died at Nagpur on 16 January 1889. I discovered this in October 2001 at the British Library, where I found the grant of probate of his will[49], as follows:

> *'Lieutenant George Roan DUNCAN, European Veteran Establishment; date of death: 16th January '89; place of death: Nagpur; probate of the will of the testator with copy of will annexed thereto; date of grant: 25th January '89; amount or value of estate: Rs 12,000; name and description of applicant: George Roan DUNCAN & Henry DUNCAN, sons of the testator and executors named in the will (dated Nagpur 26 May 1889)'.*

There is no burial record for George in the OIOC's Ecclesiastical Records, and I presume it is one of the 20% of records that slipped through the India Office's net. However, I found an official death record at the OIOC in April 2003:

> *'Lieut. George Roan Duncan; died: 16th January 1889; Nagpur; the deceased was a member of the European Volunteer Establishment; age: Ninety-four years; place of birth: Parson's Town/ Birr, Ireland;　family consists of 3 sons & 4 daughters, whose names and addresses are given below:*
>
> > *Mr G.R. Duncan, Nagpur [**George Roan DUNCAN II** (1853-1901)] (executor)*
> > *Mr H.L. Duncan, Nagpur [Henry Lauder DUNCAN (1862-1931)] (executor)*
> > *Mr J.G. Duncan, London　[John Gillespie DUNCAN (1861-aft.1903)]*
> > *Mrs L. Gordon, Simla [Mary Laura DUNCAN (1846-aft.1889[50])]*
> > *Mrs L. Blackstock, Indiana, USA [Lydia Rebecca DUNCAN (1850-1922)]*
> > *Mrs A. Eagles, Shillong, Assam [Amelia Barbara DUNCAN (1852-aft.1889[51])]*
> > *Mrs M. De La Hoyde, Nagpur [Mary Faith DUNCAN (1855-1897)]*
>
> *The property left by the deceased is in the possession of his two sons, Mr G.R. Duncan and Mr H.L. Duncan, the executors of his will of which probate has been granted'.*

The above suggests that there were no 'unfound' children. The fact that George Roan Duncan lived an age of about 90 meant that his earlier children would have been in their 60s had they survived.

No mention is made in the above record of:
> Ellen CAMPION (née DUNCAN) (1823-1851);
> Eliza CRAWLEY (née DUNCAN) (b.1841), presumably because she died before 1889;
> William George DUNCAN (1844-1872);
> Robert Roan DUNCAN (c.1849-1872).

The following is a list of George Roan Duncan's known children from his three marriages, that produced at least 47 grandchildren. Ironically, I have found only 26 great-grandchildren, whereas, it would be reasonable to expect at least 50. I suppose this is because it's very difficult to find descendants after the most recent census – 1901 in the UK.

---

[49] OIOC (L/AG/34/31/3 p.399).

[50] because she is mentioned in the 1889 death record.

[51] Ditto.

From the 1st marriage:

1. Ellen DUNCAN ^{GGA} (1823-1851) was born on 17 June 1823 at Masulipatam. She married when aged 15 ¾ , as his 2nd wife, Jeremiah CAMPION (1809-1871) at Nagpur, on 21 January 1839, and they had at least six children. She died at Mhow on 24 January 1851.

From the 2nd marriage:

2. Eliza DUNCAN ^{GGA} (1841-bef.1889) was born 15 October 1841, and baptised at Kamthi, married (1859) Theodore Lawrence CRAWLEY (c.1826-aft.1869) and had at least five children.

3. William George DUNCAN ^{GGU} (1844-1872), known as 'William', was born on 27 August 1844. He married (1868) his 1st cousin, Thomasina DUNCAN ^{1/3} (c.1848-aft.1871), had at least two children, and died of 'drink'.

4. Mary Laura DUNCAN ^{GGA} (1846-aft.1889) was born on 8 June 1846, and baptised at Kamthi. She married on 8 June 1870, William Robert Patrick GORDON (c.1842-aft.1872), and had at least two children.

5. Robert Roan DUNCAN ^{GGU} (c.1849-1872) was of 'full age' when he married Margaret Emily FOX (c.1841-aft.1869) on 5 October 1869. He had at least one child, and died of delirium tremens (alcohol poisoning).

6. Lydia Rebecca DUNCAN ^{GGA} (1850-aft.1889) was born on 11 March 1850, and baptised at Kamthi, India. She married (1881) a Canadian missionary, John BLACKSTOCK (1835-1907), and had four children, all daughters.

7. Amelia Barbara DUNCAN ^{GGA} (1852-aft.1889) was born on 16 March 1852, and baptised at Sitabuldi, near Nagpur. She married Thomas Cazaly EAGLES (? –aft.1887) and had at least three children.

8. **George Roan DUNCAN II** (1853-1901), my great-grandfather, was born on 11 November 1853, and baptised at Kamthi. He married (1874) **Mary Jane DINWIDDIE** (1848-1920), and had six children.

9. Mary Faith DUNCAN ^{GGA} (1855-1897) was born on 18 July 1855, and baptised at Sitabuldi. She married (1875) George DE LA HOYDE ^{2/3} (1851-1917) and had nine children.

From the 3rd marriage:

10. John Gillespie DUNCAN ^{GGU} (1861-aft.1903) was baptised in Madras. He married in West Ham, England in January-March 1895[52], to Selina Maud BOLITHO (c.1873-aft.1903), and had at least six children.

11. Henry Lauder DUNCAN ^{GGU} (1862-1931) was born on 1 June 1862, and baptised at Kamthi, near Nagpur. He married Kathleen Florence DILLON (c.1863/64-1935) in Sitabuldi (near Nagpur) in 1885, and they had at least three children. Henry died on 9 September 1931 at Shillong, Assam.

---

[52] Rootsweb Free BMDs (1895, Mar.; 4a, 2) and son's birth certificate.

CHAPTER 3. GEORGE ROAN DUNCAN'S 1ST MARRIAGE

Probable Marriage No.1:- was some time before 1823, to a woman named Petronella, based on the baptism record of a child named Ellen DUNCAN (see below). Petronella was probably an Indian or Anglo-Indian (Eurasian/Indo-Briton), because her daughter Ellen (see below) was described in her marriage record as an 'Indo-Briton'. George may not have married Petronella, although the record of his second marriage described him as a 'widower'. Recruits to the HEIC Army who went to India in the 18th and early 19th Centuries were encouraged to marry local women.

I have no definite information about G. R. DUNCAN I's first marriage, but it should be mentioned somewhere in his military records, and might be traced through the OIOC Ecclesiastical Records at the British Library, though I have searched in vain for it.

I've searched the OIOC marriage records in Madras Presidency (up to 1840); Bombay (to 1840), and Bengal (to 1840) without finding a marriage record, but may have missed it.

The Madras European Regiment was based in Masulipatam, Madras Presidency, in the 1820s. The place had belonged to the Dutch, who built a fort there – Fort Bandar – which was located further and further inland as the coast silted[53]. British troops were stationed there in 1820-about 1835, when Indian troops took over. For many years the local missionaries adopted unwanted babies left at their doorsteps. These girls were brought up as Christians and often married to European men. Petronella might have been one of these girls.

George had (at least) a daughter from this marriage. It seems improbable that there was only one child from the marriage/liaison, i.e. between 1823 and 1840, but I've checked all the Madras baptism records for the relevant period. It is possible that Petronella died at or near childbirth, but if so why didn't George marry again sooner?

1. Ellen DUNCAN [GGA] (1823-1851) was born on 17 June 1823 at Masulipatam. The baptism record[54] states:

> '*DUNCAN, Ellen, at Masulipatam, 22nd April 1823, daughter of George DUNCAN, Private in the M.E.* [Madras European] *Regiment, and of Petronella his wife, born 17th June 1823, was this day baptised by me, signed* [undecipherable], *Chaplain'*.

I am confident that this is 'our' George Duncan; the most compelling evidence is that Ellen's fifth child was named George Roan Duncan CAMPION (see below)! The fourth child was a son named Henry, possibly the name of the maternal grandfather. Also, a 'G.R. Duncan' was a witness at the baptism of Ellen's third child Charlotte (see below).

We can wonder why this child was named 'Ellen'. It was not a 'Duncan' name, so might have been the name of Petronella's mother.

---

[53] Pers.comm..: Bas Thyer (thyer@xtra.co.nz) 2.6.03.
[54] OIOC (N/2/8/337).

Ellen married when aged 15 ¾ , as the 2nd wife of Jeremiah CAMPION (1809-1871) at Nagpur, on 21 January 1839. The marriage record states:

> *'Nagpore; 21st January 1839; Jeremiah CAMPION, widower, Sub-Conductor, abode: Nagpore Subsdy. Force; and Ellen DUNCAN, spinster, Indo-Briton; were married by banns by me, C. Jeafferson, Chaplain, in the presence of W. Doyle, James Craig'.*

Details of the Campion family were sent to me by my 4th cousin, <u>Gordon SELLAR</u>[55], who lives near Melbourne, Australia, and who was introduced to me by Pam Botha[56], a member of the Rootsweb India list. According to a genealogy (in connection with Leitrim Castle) sent to me by Gordon Sellar, Jeremiah[57] was the son of Thomas CAMPION (1786–1833), 6th of Leitrim, and his 2nd cousin Susan CAMPION (1788-1858) (she was the daughter of Lt Jasper Campion, 38th Regiment); they were married in 1807.

Jeremiah had an elder brother, Thomas CAMPION (1808-1868), 7th of Leitrim House, who died without issue, and younger siblings as follows:

Gifford CAMPION, died young.
Henry CAMPION, died in Australia.
Rowland CAMPION (? –1861) farmed in Australia.
William Lane CAMPION, married Jane SHERROTT.
Edward CAMPION, died in the USA.
Susan CAMPION (1821-1848), married John MONSELL, and had two sons who both drowned at sea.
Emily CAMPION (c.1825-1880) married her cousin Charles Tuckey CAMPION of Dromdeer.
Sarah CAMPION, died young.
Anne CAMPION, died young.

Jeremiah was born in County Cork, Ireland, in 1809, and baptised at St Anne's Church, Shandon, Cork City, in 1810, the son of Thomas CAMPION, 6th of Leitrim House, Kilworth. He married (1st, 1828) his 1st cousin Susan BUNWORTH (? –1838) and had:

> Jeremiah CAMPION II (1829-1877) was born on 23 January 1829. He married (1857) Ellen DENEHY. He inherited the Leitrim Estate on his father's death in 1871, and sold the house and the remainder of the estate on 30 April 1875, to one of his tenants, P.Stack, who re-sold the various farms under the Irish Land Act.

Jeremiah and Ellen had (at least) a son;

> Charles Austin Bunworth CAMPION (1863-1929) who was the London Manager of the Commonwealth Bank of Australia. He married and had five sons and two daughters.

---

[55] Of 8 Lachlan Court, Werribee, Victoria 3030, Australia (tel: 03-9741-1877).

[56] <ppbotha@iprimus.com.au>

[57] He is recorded as 'Jeremy' in the document.

Note: June HEWS (née BALFOUR), granddaughter of C.A.B. Campion, of Cheltenham, is descended from this line, and knows about the court case re the Kilworth Estate (see under Henry CAMPION).

Jeremiah embarked for India with his wife and son on 6 March 1829, and landed in Madras on 16 June 1829. In addition to Jeremiah Jnr.(above) they had:

Esau CAMPION (1830- ?) was born on 14 November 1830 and died young.

Joseph CAMPION (1832- ?) was born on 19 September 1832 and died young.

Anne Wilhelmina CAMPION (1835-1866) was born on 14 February 1835. She married Dr E. MASTERS, HEIC Army, and had five sons. She died on 9 October 1866 at Vizagapatam.

Henrietta CAMPION (1837- ?) was born on 27 April 1837, and the Campion Genealogy does not record what became of her.

Ellen CAMPION (née DUNCAN), Jeremiah's 2nd wife, died at Mhow on 24 January 1851. The burial record does not give the cause of death, but it was probably from complications caused by the birth of her son George Rowen[sic] Duncan CAMPION on 2 January 1851 (see below). Ellen's burial record states[58]:

'Burials at Mhow in the Archdeaconry of Calcutta: 1851 January 24th; Ellen CAMPION, 28, Wife of Conductor Campion, Ordnance Department; buried January 25th; C.W. Cahusac, Chaplain'.

After Ellen (Jeremiah's 2nd wife) died, Jeremiah married for a 3rd time, to a widow, Amelia Matlow TARBUCK (née LLOYD). The marriage took place at Mhow on 3 September 1851, a mere eight months after his second wife died. It was quite normal in those times for men to re-marry quickly, if only to provide a mother for his children. The marriage record states[59]:

'Marriages solemnised at Mhow in the Archdeaconry of Calcutta: 1851 Septr. 3d; Jeremiah CAMPION, full age, widower, Conductor of Ordnance, Madras Establishment; abode: Mhow; father: Thomas Campion; Amelia Matlow TARBUCK, full age, widow, abode: Mhow; father: John LLOYD; by Banns; witnesses: T. Burr, R. Williams; C.W. Cahusac, Chaplain'.

In 1868, on the death of his brother Thomas, Jeremiah inherited Leitrim Castle Estate, near Kilworth, Co. Cork, Ireland, and resigned from the army.

According to the Campion Genealogy, Jeremiah died on 12 March 1871.

Jeremiah and Ellen had (at least) six children, details of them and their descendants are in Appendix A.

---

[58] OIOC (N/1/79/193).

[59] OIOC (N/1/80/101).

CHAPTER 4: GEORGE ROAN DUNCAN – THE 2ND & 3RD MARRIAGES

Marriage No.2:- George Roan DUNCAN's second marriage was on 30 December 1840, at Kamthi, near Nagpur, to a young widow named **Mary PASLEY (née LEECH)** (c.1821-1855), my 2nd great-grandmother. The marriage record[60] states:

> 'DUNCAN, George Roan; widower; Conductor of Ordnance; 30 December 1840 at Kamptee; PAISLEY [sic] Mary; widow, of Kamptee; Chaplain: Edward Whitehead; Witnesses: H. Theobald, J. Adams.

Marriage record of George Roan DUNCAN (c.1799-1889)
and Mary PASLEY (née LEECH) (c.1821-1855)

The record is signed by G.R. DUNCAN and M. PASLEY, which is the correct spelling, because it is used for her first marriage, and extensively for the children of her 1st marriage (see the chapter MARY LEECH AND THE PASLEY FAMILY). Mary must have been a European because she is described as such in the marriage record of her 1st marriage, to William PASLEY, and in the baptism record of her daughter Eliza PASLEY.

---

[60] OIOC (N/2/20/235).

Note that *'H. Theobald'* and *'J. Adams'* might be married daughters from George Duncan's first marriage, although equally they might be friends of the bride and groom.

Mary LEECH had eight children by George DUNCAN and at least three by her first husband George PASLEY. Of these 11 children, at least ten survived to be adults and married, giving her at least 41 grandchildren.

Note that Ellen DUNCAN (1823-1851), George Roan Duncan's first child, died before this marriage, having had (at least) six CAMPION children. We don't know whether the children were brought up by the grandparents, i.e. George Roan Duncan and his 2nd wife Mary, or by Jeremiah Campion and his 3rd wife – the latter is more likely.

Mary died at Sitabuldi, Nagpur, on 22 August 1855, only two weeks after the birth of her last child Mary Faith. Her burial record[61] states:

> *'2nd August 1855; Mary DUNCAN; 34 years; wife of George DUNCAN, Depty. Commissary of Ordnance, N.I. [Nagpur Irregular] Force; buried 23rd August 1855; Ward Manle(?), Catechist'.*

When Died	Christian	Surname	Age	Quality Trade or Profession &c. &c. &c.	When Buried	Signature by whom Buried
22nd August 1855	Mary	Duncan	34 Years	Wife of George Duncan, Dep. of Commissary of Ordnance N.I. Force	23rd August 1855	Ward Manle Catechist

Extract from ecclesiastical record showing burial of Mary DUNCAN (née LEECH)(c.1821-1855)

Mary was almost certainly buried at Sitabuldi or Kamthi (Kamptee), both near Nagpur, India.

George Roan DUNCAN I and Mary had at least eight children, and at least 31 grandchildren, from this 2nd marriage. Note that these children were quite young when their mother died in 1855, ranging in age from one month to 14 years. I presume they were brought up by George Duncan's 3rd wife, Alice, after his marriage to her in 1858. The youngest of the children listed below named one of her children 'Alice'.

1. Eliza DUNCAN [GGA] (1841-bef.1889) was born 15 October 1841, and baptised at Kamthi, married (1859) Theodore Lawrence CRAWLEY (c.1826-aft.1869) and had at least five children.

2. William George DUNCAN [GGU] (1844-1872), known as 'William', was born on 27 August 1844. He married (1868) his 1st cousin, Thomasina DUNCAN [1/3] (c.1848-aft.1871), had at least two children, and died of 'drink'.

---

[61] OIOC (N/2/35/92).

3. Mary Laura DUNCAN [GGA] (1846-aft.1889) was born on 8 June 1846, and baptised at Kamthi. She married on 8 June 1870, William Robert Patrick GORDON (c.1842-aft.1872), and had at least two children.

4. Robert Roan DUNCAN [GGU] (c.1849-1872) was of 'full age' when he married Margaret Emily FOX (c.1841-aft.1870) on 5 October 1869. He had at least one child, and died of delirium tremens (alcohol poisoning).

5. Lydia Rebecca DUNCAN [GGA] (1850-aft.1889) was born on 11 March 1850, and baptised at Kamthi, India. She married (1881) a Canadian missionary, John BLACKSTOCK (1835-1907), and had four daughters.

6. Amelia Barbara DUNCAN [GGA] (1852-aft.1889) was born on 16 March 1852, and baptised at Sitabuldi, near Nagpur. She married Thomas Cazaly EAGLES (? –aft.1887) and had at least three children.

7. **George Roan DUNCAN II** (1853-1901), my great-grandfather, was born on 11 November 1853, and baptised at Kamthi. He married (1874) **Mary Jane DINWIDDIE** (1848-1920), and had six children.

8. Mary Faith DUNCAN [GGA] (1855-1897) was born on 18 July 1855, and baptised at Sitabuldi. She married (1875) George DE LA HOYDE [2/3] (1851-1917) and had nine children.

It is curious that two of the above children were named 'Mary'.

Details of these children, and their offspring, follow:

1. Eliza DUNCAN [GGA] (1841-bef.1889) was born on 15 October 1841, and baptised at Kamthi, near Nagpur. The Madras Almanac (1842) reported: *"October 15 [1841] at Kamptee, the wife of Conductor G. Duncan, of a daughter"*. The baptism record[62] states:

   > 'Kamptee; 12th December 1841; Eliza, daughter of George Roan DUNCAN, Conductor of Ordnance, and Mary his wife (European), born 15 October 1841, was baptized by me (signed) Edward Whitehead, Chaplain'.

   It seems strange that Mary DUNCAN should give the name 'Eliza' to her first daughter by her second husband George DUNCAN, as this was the name of her last child by William PASLEY, her first husband, born a mere two years earlier (1839), but that Eliza might have died in infancy. Mary's persistence in naming daughters 'Eliza' suggests that her mother might have had this name, since it was not a Duncan name.

   We can presume that Eliza died before 1889, because she is not listed as one of George Roan Duncan's surviving children when he died in that year (see above).

   Eliza married Theodore Lawrence CRAWLEY (c.1826-aft.1873), son of John Percival Crawley, on 20 July 1859 at Sitabuldi, when she was 17. He was an administrative official (uncovenanted) in the HEIC. He was Extra Assistant Commissioner at Sumbalpore, Central Provinces (on leave) in 1869, at Raepore (Raipur?), Central Provinces, in 1870, and at

---

[62] OIOC (N/2/20/376).

Mundla, Central Provinces, in 1871-1873, but not in 1874[63]. I could find no burial record in Bengal in 1873-1875 (incl.), and wonder whether he returned to the UK.

The marriage record[64] states:

> 'Seetabuldee; 20th July 1859; Theodore Lawrence CRAWLEY, 33, widower, Offg.Asst. Commissioner; abode: Seetabuldee; father: John Percival Crawley; and Eliza DUNCAN, 17, spinster, abode: Seetabuldee, father: George Roan Duncan; by licence; witnesses: G. R. Duncan [bride's father], H [?]. J. Laville, M. Laville; H. P. James, Chaplain'

Names on baptism records are often difficult to decipher; the LAVILLE witnesses were probably Francis James and Maria (née PASLEY) (see the Chapter on Mary Leech and the Pasley Family.

Note that a John Percival CRAWLEY was born on 16 January 1821, and baptised at Cawnpore[65]. He was probably the elder brother of Theodore, having the same name as Theodore's father (see marriage record below).

The 1881 Census shows a Percival CRAWLEY (b.c.1826), born Cawnpore, living at 13 Smith Street, Lambeth, occupation: 'Opium Department (CS)' [Civil Service?], and his wife Elizabeth, son Chas St. Clair CRAWLEY (b.c.1853) born at Quilon, India, an artist, and daughter Mary Elizabeth CRAWLEY (b.c.1865) born at Islington. Percival was almost certainly Theodore's brother.

If Theodore and Eliza returned to England, their deaths may be in Free BMDs and their Wills may be in the PRO.

Theodore and Eliza had at least five children:

a. Percival Duncan CRAWLEY [1/2] (1860-1867) was born on 5 August 1860 and baptised at Sitabuldi[66]:

> 'Baptisms solemnised at Seetabuldee: baptised: 2nd December 1860; born: 5th August 1860; Percival Duncan, son of Theodore Lawrence and Eliza CRAWLEY; abode: Seetabuldee; rank etc.: Extra Assistant Commissioner, Nagpore; J.G. Cooper [Minister]'.

I presume he was named after his two grandfathers, and his uncle Percival CRAWLEY (c.1826-aft.1881)(see above).

Percival died, aged seven years, on 25 November 1867, and was buried at Raipur[67]:

> 'Burials at Kamptee: (copy of Return of a burial at Raipore; 1867 November 25th; Percival CRAWLEY; 7 years 2 months; [no entry under parents]; bu. 26

---

[63] Thacker's Gazette.

[64] OIOC (N/2/40/184).

[65] OIOC (N/1/11/642).

[66] OIOC (N/2/41/254).

[67] OIOC (N/1/122/132).

November 1867; cause: Epileptic fits; Ennis (?) Twyford, Dy. Comr. [Deputy Commissioner]'.

b. <u>Emily Maria CRAWLEY</u> [1/2] (1862- ?) was born on 29 August 1862, and baptised at Sitabuldi. The baptism record[68] states:

> *'Baptisms solemnised at Seetabuldee; baptised: 4th January 1863; born: 29th April 1862; Emily Maria, daughter of Theodore Lawrence and Eliza CRAWLEY; abode: Seetabuldee; rank etc.: Extra Assistant Commissioner, Central Provinces; Stephen Hislop'.*

We don't know if Emily survived infancy, or, if so, where she might have married.

I suspect that 'Emily' was the name of the paternal grandmother, i.e. Theodore Crawley's mother. 'Maria' may have been the name of the maternal grandmother, i.e. Mary Leech's mother.

c. <u>Mary Laura CRAWLEY</u> [1/2] (1864- ?) was born on 15 December 1864, and baptised at Jabalpur, W. Bengal[69].

> *'Baptisms solemnized at Jubbulpore: 1865 December 4th; born: 1864 December 15th; Mary Laura, daughter of Theodore Lawrence & Eliza CRAWLEY; abode: Jubbulpore; Extra Assistant Commissioner; C.W, Cahusac, Chaplain'.*

Note that a 'Mary A. CRAWLEY' b. East Indies, age 37, was living at 1 Stannage, Southwark, with an uncle, James Caird, in the 1901 Census. However, the second initial is wrong, and Crawley is a quite common name.

d. <u>Minnie Pauline CRAWLEY</u> [1/2] (1867- ?) was born on 2 January 1867, and baptised at Kamthi[70]:

> *'Baptisms solemnised at Kamptee: 8th May 1867; born: 2d January 1867; Minnie Pauline, daughter of Theodore Lawrence and Eliza CRAWLEY; abode: Seetabuldee, Nagpore; rank etc.: Extra Assistant Commissioner; Rev'd. John G. Cooper'.*

No record of a marriage in England has been found.

---

[68] OIOC (N/2/44/59).

[69] OIOC (N/1/114/228).

[70] OIOC (N/2/48/134).

e. William Charles CRAWLEY [1/2] (1869- ?) was born on 23 May 1869 and baptised at Nagpur:

> *'Baptisms solemnised at Nagpore: baptised 8th August 1869; born: 23rd May 1869; William Charles, son of Theodore Lawrence and Eliza CRAWLEY; abode: Sitabuldi, Nagpore; rank etc.: Extra Assistant Commissioner, Nagpore; J.G. Cooper (Rev'd.)'.*

A William Charles CRAWLEY married at Ely in the June quarter of 1894[71], who may be 'our' William.

2. William George DUNCAN [GGU] (1844-1872), known as 'William', was born on 27 August 1844. He is referred to in the letter from (William) Robert DUNCAN [2GGU] (George Roan DUNCAN I's brother) dated 13 March 1867: *"I am glad to hear that your son William is such a fine young man...."*. He appears in his marriage record as 'George William DUNCAN' (see below).

William was the first known son of George Roan Duncan, and I have no doubt he was christened 'William' in honour of his paternal grandfather, and 'George' in honour of his father.

From 'Baptisms solemnised at the Chaplain's Station within the Archdeaconry of Madras':

> *'William George DUNCAN; baptised on: 15 September 1844; said to be born: 27 August 1844; son of George Roan and Mary DUNCAN; parents' abode: Nagpore; father's profession: Conductor on Depot'[72].*

William became a railway policeman at Sitabuldi (marriage record) and at Mundlah (burial record). He married his 1st cousin, Thomasina DUNCAN [1/3] (c.1848-aft.1870), daughter of his uncle Robert (see Chapter 1 The Early Duncans). The marriage record[73] states:

> *'25 February 1868, George William DUNCAN, aged 23, bachelor, Inspector of Railway Police, abode: Seetabuldee, father: George Roan Duncan; and Thomasina DUNCAN, aged 20, spinster, abode: Seetabuldee, father: Robert Duncan; witnesses: G.R. Duncan [presumably George Roan Duncan, the father], and W.R. Duncan; Chaplain: Thomas A. Pratt'.*

I wonder whether the *'W. R. Duncan'* listed as a witness was the bride's father, who may thus have been 'William Robert DUNCAN'. If so, he might have escorted his daughter from Ireland to India for the wedding. This would also explain why we can't find a 'William' among the children of old William DUNCAN. He might have been called 'Robert' to avoid confusion with his father, as was common practice. There are no other W.R. Duncans in my records.

---

[71] Rootsweb, Free BMDs (June 1894, 3b, 939).
[72] OIOC (N/2/22/124).
[73] OIOC (N/1/124/102).

William George was buried at Jabalpur, now in Madhya Pradesh State, having died on 10 February 1872, less than four years after he married. The burial record[74] states:

'Burials at Jubbulpore; 1872 February 10th; William DUNCAN, 26, Inspector of Police (at Mundlah); buried: 1872 February 11th; cause of death: Drink; E. Champion, Missy. CMS [Church Missionary Society]'. 'Mundlah' is now Mandla, near Jabalpur.

Thomasina might have re-married in England after the early death of her husband, when she was only about 24 (see under her name in Chapter 1: The Early Duncans).

William and Thomasina had at least two children, 'discovered' by me in 2001:

a. <u>Anna Mary DUNCAN</u> [1/2] (1869- ?) was born on 5 June 1869 and baptised at Sitabuldi, near Nagpur. The baptism record[75] states:

> *'Baptisms solemnized at All Saints Church, Seetabuldee; 1869 July 14th; born: 1869 June 5th; Anna Mary, daughter of William George & Thomasina DUNCAN; Godparents: George Duncan* [Grandfather], *Eliza Crawley* [Aunt, see above], *Maria Margaret Pasley* [Aunt]*; abode: Seetabuldee; father's occupation: Insptr.Police; G. T. Carruthers, MA, Chaplain of Nagpore'*.

I suggest that the name 'Anna' honours Thomasina's mother Ann(a) DUNCAN (née WOODLOCK), and the second name 'Mary' honours the paternal grandmother, Mary DUNCAN (née LEECH).

If Anna Mary's widowed mother Thomasina married in England in 1883, she would probably have taken her children with her, so Anna Mary may have married in England.

b. <u>George Roan DUNCAN III</u> [1/2] (1870- ?) was born on 25 July 1870 and baptised at Jabalpur. He was the third Duncan to be named 'George Roan', following my great-great-grandfather (**G. R. Duncan I**), and my great-grandfather (**G. R. Duncan II**). The baptism record[76] states:

> *'Baptisms solemnised at Jabalpur, Central Provinces; baptized: 1871 January 29th; born: 1870 July 25th; George Roan, son of William John* [sic] *& Thomasina DUNCAN; abode: Mundla; father's occupation: Police Inspector; W. B. Drawbridge, Senior Chaplain'*.

He may have gone to England with his mother before 1883. A George DUNCAN, 26, (b.1875) was recorded in the 1901 Census, a police constable in Dover, Kent.

---

[74] OIOC (N/1/139/134).

[75] OIOC (N/1/129/54).

[76] OIOC (N/1/135/34).

3. Mary Laura DUNCAN [GGA] (1846-aft.1889) was 'discovered' by me in 2000. She was born on 8 June 1846 and baptised at Kamthi, India, within the Archdeaconry of Madras[77]:

> *'Mary Laura, baptised 26 August 1846, born 8 June 1846, daughter of George and Mary DUNCAN; abode: Kamptee; occupation of father: Conductor of Ordnance; was baptised by me, John McEvoy, MA, in the presence of us: G. Duncan [father], Jane Smith, Mary Duncan [mother]'.*

I wonder who Jane Smith was? A friend, or might she have been a married daughter from George Duncan's first marriage?

We know that Mary Laura lived until 1889, because she is listed in her father's death record of that year[78].

I discovered in April 2003 that she married, on 8 June 1870, at All Saints Church, Sitabuldi, William Robert Patrick GORDON (c.1842-aft.1898), son of William Ebenezer Gordon[79]:

> *'Marriages solemnized at All Saints Church, Seetabuldee: 1870 June 8th; William Robert Patrick GORDON; 28; Bachelor; Accountant in Public Works Department; abode: Seetabuldee; father: William Ebenezer Gordon; Mary Laura DUNCAN; 24; Spinster; abode: Seetabuldee; father: George Roan Duncan; by Licence; witnesses: G.R. Duncan [father], L.R. Duncan [sister Lydia Rebecca], G.R. Duncan [brother George Roan]; G.T. Carruthers, MA, Chaplain of Seetabuldee'.*

The following information was given to me by Gay Guegan[80], and is included here to make it easier to identify various members of the Gordon family.

William Ebenezer's father was Robert GORDON (1800-1853), who married in Calcutta. His father was Adam GORDON (b.c.1760, in Scotland) of the 73rd Regiment, who married in Cawnpore (1787), Susanna, a native woman. Adam died on 17 July 1834, and Susanna on 19 May 1826.

Robert GORDON was born on 29 September 1800 in Calcutta. He married twice.

His first wife was Mary CARPENTER, and they had the following children:
Adam Robert GORDON (1821-1884)
William Ebenezer GORDON (1821-1885) – the groom's father.
James Money GORDON
Martha Susanna Margaret GORDON (1829-1862)

Robert Gordon's second wife was Sophia Gazelle LISH, and they had the following children:
Gazelle Sophia GORDON (1833?-1915)
Alexander Lish GORDON (1834-1838)
Hannah Mercy GORDON (1835-1914?)
Felix GORDON (1837-1838)

---

[77] OIOC (N/2/25/275).

[78] OIOC (L/AG/34/14A/271).

[79] OIOC (N/1/132/107).

[80] ROLY@Guegan.fslife.co.uk

Phoebe Marah GORDON (1838-1910)
Benjamin Dukoff GORDON (1841-1926), the grandfather of Gay Guegan.
Pauline Ruth GORDON (1845?-1914)
Caleb Mack GORDON (1846?-1868)

William Ebenezer GORDON (1821-1885), the groom's father, served in the Madras Volunteer Guards (1861) having previously volunteered in the Agra Militia at the time of the Mutiny, and took part in a battle near Agra on 5 July 1857[81]. He had a recorded wife (married 2nd October 1840, Agra) named Eveline (or Evelina) REID (1822- ?)[82]. His 2nd wife was named Elizabeth ….(1832-1855); she was born in Sermapore, India, on 18 September 1832, and died in Agra on 11 February 1855, aged 22 years and 4 months. From the date of birth of her son Ebenezer (see below), it seems likely that Elizabeth died of complications from childbirth.

They had an infant son:

Ebenezer Samuel GORDON (1855-1856), born on 5 February 1855, and died on 21 February 1856.

Note that an Ebenezer GORDON married Jessy JONES in 1854 (N/2/33/459, reg.1,13,815).

'Our' William Robert Patrick GORDON was an accountant in the Public Works Department (PWD), and presumably an uncovenanted civil servant. It should be possible to trace his stations through the almanacs and civil lists, but only the pension records will indicate children. We know that he lived until 1898 because he was a witness at the marriage of his son, William Duncan GORDON.

Note that W.R.P. Gordon had a brother, Cuthbert Henry GORDON (b.c.1872), who married W.R.P.'s niece, Mary Alison EAGLES, daughter of Thomas Cazaly Eagles and his wife Amelia Barbara (née Duncan, sister of Mary Laura Duncan) (see below).

Mary Laura and William had at least two children:

a. <u>William Duncan GORDON</u> [1/2] (1871-1920) was almost certainly the first child. Although technically possible, it's unlikely that there was a child born before him. He was born on 2 November 1871 and baptised at Sitabuldi on the same day as his cousin Mary Moss PASLEY[83]:

'Baptisms solemnized at All Saints Church, Seetabuldee: 1873 April 24th; born: 1871 November 2nd; William Duncan, Son of William Robert Patrick and Mary Laura GORDON; abode: Seetabuldee; occ.: Accountant, P.W.D.; G.F. Carruthers, M.A., Chaplain of Seetabuldee; Godparents: Charles Augustus William Jackson, George Roan Duncan, Maria Elizabeth Pasley'.

---

[81] SKELTON, Constance & BULLOCH, John, 'Gordons under Arms', The New Sporting Club, Aberdeen.

[82] E-mail from Gay Guegan (12.11.04).

[83] OIOC (N/1/144/56).

I do not know the Jackson godparent. 'George Roan Duncan' might be the child's grandfather, or his uncle. 'Maria Elizabeth Pasley' is the daughter-in-law of the child's grandmother (see Mary Leech and the Pasley Family).

William Duncan GORDON became a bombardier in the Royal Artillery (see marriage record below), and it is possible that his military record might be at the PRO or OIOC.

A William D. GORDON, who is surely the same person, died on 7 February 1920[84]:

> 'Burials at All Saints Church, Lucknow: 1920 February 7th; William GORDON; 49 years; Lieutenant S & T Corps; buried: 1920 Feb. 8th; cause: pneumonia; Ronald Irwin, Garrison Chaplain'.

He was also listed as 'Lt. W. D. GORDON, Supply and Transport Corps, of Indian nationality, died on 7 February 1920, and was buried at Lucknow Cantonment Military Cemetery'.

He married, on 3 January 1898 at Agra, Marie Kathleen DE BRETTON (c.1870-aft.1898), daughter of Charles James De Bretton[85]:

> 'Marriages solemnized at St George's Church, Agra: 1898 Jany. 3rd; William Duncan GORDON; 26; Bachelor; Bombr. 11th F.B. [Field Battery?], R.A. [Royal Artillery]; abode: Agra; father: William Robert Patrick Gordon; and Marie Kathleen DE BRETTON; 28; Spinster; abode: Rutlam; father: Charles James De Bretton; by Licence; witnesses: Geo. Bailey, Captn.; W.R.P. Gordon [father of the groom]; Charles A. Mason, Chaplain'.

The birth of a child named William Duncan GORDON was registered in Portsea, Hampshire, in the March Quarter of 1898[86], but this could not be a child of the above marriage.

I posted a message to the India Rootsweb List asking if anyone knew of descendants of the Gordon-De Bretton marriage. I received a reply from Pam Peisley of Didcot, to the effect that she knew of a John and Alastair DE BRETTON-GORDON in Dehra Dun, India, and subsequently in England in the 1950s, but had since lost touch. It's possible that the descendants of William and Marie's marriage (above) did a 'reverse hyphenation' of their surnames.

b. Evelina Mary Lydia GORDON [1/2] (1873- ?) was almost certainly the second child, born on 16 May 1873 and baptised at Sitabuldi[87]. She must have been named after her paternal grandmother, Eveline(a) REID.

---

[84] OIOC (N/1/443/251).

[85] OIOC (N/1/264/248).

[86] Free BMDs, Portsea (2b, 475).

[87] OIOC (N/1/146/65).

'Baptisms solemnized at All Saints Church, Seetabuldee: 1873 December 20th; 1873 May 16th; Evelina Mary Lydia, Daughter of William Robert Patrick and Mary Laura GORDON;abode: Seetabuldee; occ.: Accountant, P.W.D.; G. F. Carruthers, M.A., Chaplain, Seetabuldee; Godparents: George William Pasley, Lydia Rebecca Duncan, Amelia Barbara Duncan'.

The godfather 'George William PASLEY' is the half-brother of the child's mother. The godmothers, 'Lydia Rebecca Duncan' and 'Amelia Barbara Duncan', are the child's aunts.

4. <u>Robert Roan DUNCAN</u> ^{GGU} (c.1848-1872) was 'discovered' by me in April 2001, through his marriage record[88] at OIOC. I don't yet know his year of birth, though he was of 'full age' when he married in 1869, and he was 23 when he died in 1872. I have placed him in a gap between Mary Laura and Lydia Rebecca.

Robert became an accountant in the Civil Commissioner's office.

He married, on 5 October 1869 at Kamthi, Margaret Emily FOX (c.1841-aft.1876), daughter of John Fox, who was probably in military service.

'5th October 1869, Robert Roan DUNCAN, age: full; Acct. in Commissioner's office; abode: Nagpore; father's name: George Roan Duncan; and Margaret Emily FOX; age: 18; abode: Kamptee; father's name: John Fox; married by licence; witnesses: A. Scott, Mary E. Scott; William H. Gale, Chaplain'.

The witness 'A. Scott' might have been Ann SCOTT, mother of Christiana SCOTT, who married Thomas PRITCHARD (see THE PRITCHARDS). However, they are more likely to be relatives of the bride.

Robert died on 31 March 1872, a mere 2 ½ years after his marriage, and was buried at Sitabuldi, Nagpur. The burial record[89] states:

'Burials at Seetabuldee; 1872 March 31st; Robert Roan DUNCAN; 23 years; Accountant C Co's [Civil Commissioner's] Office; buried: 1872 March 31st; cause of death: Delirium Tremens; G.F. Carruthers, MA, Chaplain of Seetabuldee'.

Robert and Margaret had at least one child (I have found no record of any earlier child):

a. <u>George William Roan DUNCAN</u> ^{1/2} (1872-1872) was born on 20 February 1872, a little over a month before his father died. He was baptised at Sitabuldi, near Nagpur[90]:

'Baptisms solemnised at All Saints Church, Seetabuldee; 1872 March 18th; born: 1872 February 20th; George William Roan, son of Robert Roan & Margaret Emily DUNCAN, Godparents: George Roan Duncan [grandfather], Robert Roan Duncan [father], Lydia Rebecca Duncan [aunt], abode:

---

[88] OIOC (N/1/130/105).

[89] OIOC (N/1/139/153).

[90] OIOC (N/1/139/66).

Seetabuldee; father's occupation: Accountant; G. T. Carruthers, MA, Chaplain of Seetabuldee'.

The child died at Sitabuldi in 1872, about four months after the death of his father. The burial record[91] states:

> *'Burials at Seetabuldee: 1872 July 18th, William George DUNCAN, age: 5 months; son of Robert Roan DUNCAN, Accountant C Cy (?) Office (deceased); buried 1872 July 18th; cause of death: Diarrhea; G.F. Carruthers, Chaplain of Seetabuldee'.*

David Dinwiddie, in a letter to General Blake dated 2 March 1875, wrote: *"You are right about Foxe's daughter. She is the widow of the late William Duncan, brother to George, Jane's 'Gude Man'. I hope Jane will have better luck than she had - poor girl."* I think David Dinwiddie must have had his names wrong, but this snippet gives a clue that Margaret came from a military family.

It is worth noting that a John DUNCAN married a Margaret FOX in Madras in 1825 (N/2/10/276).

Margaret Emily DUNCAN (née FOX) re-married about four years later, on 11 August 1876 at Trichinopoly, as I discovered from an entry in the Madras Almanac[92]:

> *'MOORE-DUNCAN – At Trichinopoly, Mr C.H. Moore, to M.E. widow of the late Mr R.R. DUNCAN, August 11'.*

I have not made any effort to trace 'C.H. Moore', nor the possible children (if any), because they would not be related to us.

5. Lydia Rebecca DUNCAN [GGA] (1850-1922) was 'discovered' by me in April 2001. She was born on 11 March 1850, and baptised at Kamthi, near Nagpur, India[93]. I feel sure that her second name honours her paternal grandmother **Rebecca DUNCAN**. It may be that 'Lydia' was the maternal grandmother's name (i.e. Lydia LEECH), but the child also had an aunt named Lydia (George Roan Duncan's sister).

> *'Lydia Rebecca, at the Chaplain's Station within the Diocese of Madras, baptised 16 June 1850, born 11 March 1850, daughter of George and Mary DUNCAN, abode: Kamptee; occupation: Conductor of Ordnance; Warner B. Ottley, Chaplain; witnesses: G.R. Duncan* [father], *for R. Duncan* [Rebecca or Robert Duncan?], *Mary Duncan* [mother] *for R. Duncan, Maria Pasley* [step-sister].

The witness 'Maria Pasley' was Maria PASLEY [GGA] a child of Mary Duncan's first marriage (see: Mary Leech and the Pasley Family), and thus the bride's step-sister, then aged 14.

---

[91] OIOC (N/1/141/171).

[92] OIOC, Asylum Press Almanac (Madras) 1877.

[93] OIOC (N/2/29/222).

Lydia's marriage, in Nagpur on 3 January 1881, to a Canadian Methodist minister, John BLACKSTOCK (1835-1907), eldest son of John Blackstock, was discovered by me in 2002.

The marriage record[94] states:

> 'Marriages solemnised in the C.P. [Central Provinces]: 1881 Jany. 3*rd*; John BLACKSTOCK; age: 46; Bachelor; rank etc.: Minister; abode: Nagpur; father: John Blackstock; and Lydia DUNCAN; age: 30; Spinster; abode: Nagpur; father: Geo. R. Duncan; witnesses: William R.G. Gordon, Louis(e) M. Gordon; Rev. D.A. Fox, Minister, Methodist Specified Church, Nagpur'.

The witness 'William R.G. Gordon' must be William Robert Patrick GORDON, the bride's brother-in-law, married to Mary Laura DUNCAN (1846-aft.1889). The other Gordon witness might be his brother, sister, or wife.

I discovered[95] that John Blackstock was born on 8 September 1835 at Essa Township, Simcoe County, Ontario, Canada, and was a pastor of Oldham Methodist Church, Bombay in 1876-79, Poona (1879), Nagpur (1879-1880), and Poona (1884-1887). In Thacker's Directory he is recorded in Poona (Pune) in 1879, and in 1884 at the Methodist Episcopal Mission. He was the eldest son of John Blackstock, farmer (b.8 May 1807, Ryefield Townland, Co. Cavan, Ireland; d. 4 Jan 1884, Essa Township, Simcoe, Ontario, Canada), and Anne Grant (b.c.1805, Ireland; d.23 Nov 1890, Essa Township). They were a Scots-Irish-Canadian family that was documented by Ordella Park who recently published a book on this family (*George, John, William & Moses Blackstock of County Cavan, Ireland*, Rexburg, Idaho, 1999).

The Blackstock family (John, Lydia, Isabella and Anna) went to the US on 25 March 1887, when John retired under a doctor's certificate[96]. They returned to India on 2 November 1889. John was appointed to the Boys Orphanage, Lodipur, Shahjahanpur in January 1890. His obituary described him as 'A man of magnificent physical proportions and strength, nothing seemed too hard for him to undertake, and so well preserved was he that only very recently his friends had noticed he had begun to fail'[97].

John Blackstock (1834-1907) died on 1 July 1907 in a sanatorium in Naini Tal, India[98].

The following information comes from DePauw University Archives and Special Collections; *The Encyclopedia of World Methodism, Vol. 1*; and *History of Methodist Missions of the Methodist Episcopal Church, Vol. III, Widening Horizons 1845-1895*:

> *'John was a school teacher in Simcoe Co., Ontario, before going to Greencastle, Indiana to attend DePauw University. It is likely that his great uncle, the Reverend Moses Blackstock who lived in Indiana, had influenced his decision. Since young John wanted to be a minister it was likely that he was advised to attend DePauw University and Theological School. He was in that school's records. His grades for his senior year of 1871-1872 were very high.*

---

[94] OIOC (N/11/7/1491).

[95] Through Doug Blackstock of Auckland, NZ (<doug.blstock@xtra.co.nz>).

[96] Missonary Society return from John Blackstock on 3 August 1896 (from Buck Crist).

[97] Kankab Hind (4 July 1907).

[98] E-mail from Buck Crist: Jan 2006.

The lowest was 90! The records from DePauw University also tracked his career as a minister - first serving in Indiana and then going to India in 1875. Except for visits to the Western Hemisphere, he remained in India the rest of his life. Besides being a minister, he helped manage an orphanage, was in charge of the city high school at Shahjahanpur, and was a chaplain to some troops stationed nearby. His wife Lydia (Duncan) Blackstock founded four girls' schools in Poona and supervised them for about a year. Her greatest task was assisting her husband with the orphanage at Shahjahanpur for 18 years'.

'J. Blackstock' is recorded in Blacker's Directory of 1905 as *'revd, missionary, M.E. Mission, Shahjahanpur'*. 'L. Blackstock' is recorded as *'Mrs, Suptdt. of city and zen. work, M.E. Mission, Lodipore, Shajahanpur'*.

Lydia BLACKSTOCK (née DUNCAN) (1850-1922) died on 1 May 1922 at Bareilly Mission Hospital, India[99]. She had continued the work of her husband after he died, and later at Bareilly and Hardoi as a lady missionary

Ordella Park also mentions a letter (1971) from Barbara Blackstock Cody of Toronto:

> *'Nevertheless as late as 1905 or so, I saw someone on the street so like my Uncle George Tate Blackstock that I said to my mother, "Who on earth is that living image of Uncle George?" And she replied, "He is Mr John Blackstock, a Methodist minister just back from India". He had been there as a full time missionary for many years. Subsequently, I was able to link that up with the pictures of two little girls whose pictures I had seen in a desk at my Grandma Blackstock's. On asking about them, I had been told that their father was a missionary in India. Later still, not so many years ago (ten or so [i.e. c.1950]) I was able to establish for the Indian Government after Great Britain had given India its independence - that two older women who had been born in India and wished to stay on for the rest of their lives, were undoubtedly descended from those Blackstocks who settled near Barrie and were therefore of British descent and eligible to receive pensions from the Government of India, which were made to such'.*

In her father's death record[100], Lydia is recorded as *'Mrs L. Blackstock, Indiana, USA'*, which suggests that the Blackstocks returned temporarily to the USA before 1889, and some remained there.

Lydia and John had four daughters. Curiously, there are no baptism records for the three girls who were born in India in the OIOC ecclesiastical records.

  a. <u>Isabella Thoburn BLACKSTOCK</u> [1/2] (1882-1975) was born in Madras[101] on 4 December 1882[102]. She was mentioned by her sister Constance when the latter entered the USA through Ellis Island in 1923: *"She was joining her sister Mrs Isabella Beardsley at 199 E. Maple Ave., Bound Brook, NJ"[103]*. She taught in India and came to the US on a sabbatical, where she met her future husband when she

---

[99] Ordella Park (via Doug Blackstock).

[100] OIOC (L/AG/34/14A/271).

[101] Missonary Society return from John Blackstock on 20 January 1905 (from Buck Crist).

[102] Missonary Society return from John Blackstock on 3 August 1896 (from Buck Crist).

[103] e-mail from Doug Blackstock (14.4.2003; <doug.blstock@xtra.nz>).

travelled to Derby, CT, to speak to a Methodist women's missionary society; she is believed to have returned to India only once, when she took her son and daughter there (in about 1921)[104].

She died on 15 October 1975[105] in Hillsborough Township, Somerset County, NJ[106]; she was aged 93[107]. Her date of birth was recorded as 4 December 1882, although the 1920 Census records her as 34 in 1920, and therefore born in about 1886. Her social security number was SSN 142-54-8379, issued in New Jersey in 1972.

Isabel married (c.1914) Alling Prudden BEARDSLEY (1877-1950)[108], born on 29 January 1877 at Derby, New Haven, CT[109], the son of Dr George Lucius Beardsley and Louise/Louisa Marie/Maria Alling.

Alling Beardsley was recorded in the 1920 Census as aged 40, and therefore born in about 1880, a chemist, working in a chemical factory in Bound Brook, NJ (Calco - now part of Union Cyanamid). He was recorded in the 1930 Federal Census[110], aged 53, living at 1414, Evergreen Avenue, Plainfield, Union County, NJ. He died on 23 September 1950[111].

Isabel and Alling had at least two children, twins[112]:

i) <u>Alling Prudden BEARDSLEY II</u> **2/1** (1915-1989), SSN: 156-09-0058), known as 'Bud', was born in Derby, Connecticut[113] on 7 January 1915, and was recorded as four years and eleven months old in the 1920 US Census, and a twin of his sister Carol(ine) (see below). He was also recorded, aged 15, in the 1930 Federal Census. Alling and Carol moved with their parent to New Jersey, where Alling II graduated from high school in Plainfield, and from Wesleyan University, Middleton, CT (1938), and took a Masters degree from NY University (1939?). He joined Montgomery Ward where he met his future wife. Following Pearl Harbor he volunteered, was commissioned in the US Army and sent overseas in early 1944, to India, then Burma. He served with the 5307 Composite Unit (Merrill's Marauders), and guarded an airfield at Myitkina. He contracted malaria and convalesced in India, later returning to Burma. While in India he visited his two aunts, Anna and Esther Blackstock.

After the War he remained in the Army Reserve, retiring as a Lieut. Colonel. He had a retail hardware and wholesale industrial supply

---

104 E-mail from Mary Louise Beardsley (mlbeardslet@earthlink.net) 28.12.04.

105 E-mail from Buck Crist: Jan 2006.

106 E-mail from Buck Crist: Jan 2006.

107 E-mail from Mary Louise Beardsley (mlbeardslet@earthlink.net) 28.12.04.

108 1920 US Census.

109 LDS Familysearch website.

110 Roll T626_1388, p.88.

111 Ibid.

112 1920 US Census.

113 1920 US Census.

business. He died on 10 October 1989, but unfortunately the US Social Security Death Index does not record where.

Alling married on 5 October 1942 at Fort Benning, GA to Carol Elizabeth ROSSITER (1918-2002) and had three children[114]:

> Suzanne Winton BEARDSLEY [3] (b.1943) was born on 28 September 1943[115]. She married Thomas J. ALBANI and has two children.

> Alling P. BEARDSLEY III [3] (b.1944) was born on 6 October 1944. He and Betty P. Beardsley live at 1800 Charlie Ennis Road, Dyersburg, TN 38024 (tel: 731-285-0968)[116]. I wrote to him (without reply) on 1 May 2004. They have one child:

> Mary Louise BEARDSLEY [3] (b.1954) was born on 20 April 1954. She married Kent Allen KELLEY, has two adopted children, and lives in Eden Prairie, MI, a suburb of Minneapolis[117]. I've exchanged a few messages with Mary Louise and have sent her information.

ii) Carolyn Alling BEARDSLEY [2/1] (1915-2004) was born on 7 January 1915 in Connecticut, and was recorded as 'Caroline', four years and eleven months old in the 1920 US Census, and a twin of her brother Alling. She was also recorded as 'Carolyn', aged 15, in the 1930 Federal Census. She married Buckley CRIST (1913-1977) in 1937 in Plainfield, and had two children[118]. She died on 2 April 2004 in Plainfield.

> Peter Beardsley CRIST [3] (1943-1977) married Agnes Szanto; he died in the 1970s; he had one child.

> Buckley CRIST II [3] (b.1944), known as 'Buck', married Susan Belvin BOWERS; they have two children[119].

b. Anna Grant BLACKSTOCK [1/2] (1885-aft.1950) was born in Nagpur[120] on 18 December 1885[121]. She went to the USA for education in 1903 and received a degree from Lasell College in 1906. She returned to India and probably became a missionary, at Budaun, UP (see below). We know she lived until 1923, because she was mentioned by her sister Constance when she entered the USA on 17 April 1923.

---

[114] E-mail from Mary Louise Beardsley (mlbeardslet@earthlink.net) 28.12.04.

[115] E-mail from Buck Crist: Jan 2006.

[116] Ancestry.com

[117] 18323 Bearpath Trail, Eden Prairie, Minnesota 55347; (952) 974-0187

[118] E-mail from Mary Louise Beardsley (mlbeardslet@earthlink.net) 28.12.04.

[119] Buckley Crist, 317 Woodlawn Avenue, Glencoe, IL 60022 (b-crist@northwestern.edu).

[120] IGI Film # 6142799.

[121] E-mail from Buck Crist: Jan 2006.

She remained in India all her life working as a WFMS missionary, and died before 1954 (when Mary Louise Beardsley was born).

c. <u>Esther Duncan BLACKSTOCK</u> ^{1/2} (1888-1942/1954)[122] was born in Romney, IN, USA, on 27 March 1888[123], while her father was on sick leave. She went to the USA in 1904 for education, but returned to India and remained there for the rest of her life working as a WFMS missionary. She died before 1954 (when Mary Louise Beardsley was born).

d. <u>Constance Ella BLACKSTOCK</u> ^{1/2} (1891-1975) was born in Shahjahanpur on 12 April 1891[124]. She graduated from Lasell College in 1909, and subsequently taught there in the 1930s. She did missionary work in India, but returned to the US. An informant says: *"She was recorded arriving in New York on 19 March 1907 on the SS* Caledonia *out of Glasgow. Described as a 16 year old student and a US citizen. Last residence in US was recorded as Auburndale(?), Mass. and she stated that she was going home to the same place. (That part of the entry was difficult to read but it looks like the name Russell Sing(?) is recorded in connection to her home)"*. Also: *"...arriving in New York on 17 April 1923 on the SS Assyria from Glasgow. She was described as 32 years old* [which would make her year of birth c.1891], *single, and a missionary. Her last residence was Hardoi, India, and her nearest relative in India was Miss A. Blackstock* [presumably Anna], *of Budaun, U.P. Her fare was paid by the Women's Foreign Missionary Society. She declared that she had previously been in the USA in 1915, and was intending to stay permanently in the US". "She was recorded as born in Shahjahanpur, India, and her nationality is stated (curiously) as 'Scotch'"*. [Ellis Island records][125].

The 1930 Census shows a Constance BLACKSTOCK, age 38 (therefore born c.1892), born in India, who was teaching at Newton, Middlesex County, MA. I feel confident this is 'our' Constance.

Constance died aged 84 in November 1975 at Ocean Grove, NJ. Her date of birth was given as 12 April 1891. She was unmarried[126].

6. <u>Amelia Barbara DUNCAN</u> ^{GGA} (1852-aft.1889) was born on 16 March 1852, and baptised at Sitabuldi, near Nagpur, India. I 'discovered' her through a letter[127] written by David Dinwiddie: *"...little Mary[128] is now playing with her Aunt Miss Amelia Duncan who is with us spending a few days from Nagpore..."*. The Dinwiddies were living in Kamthi at the

<hr>

[122] ibid.

[123] Missionary Society return from John Blackstock 3 August 1896.

[124] US Social Security Death Index; Missionary Society return from John Blackstock 3 August 1896.

[125] e-mail from Doug Blackstock (14.4.2003; <doug.blstock@xtra.nz>).

[126] E-mail from Mary Louise Beardsley (mlbeardslet@earthlink.net) 28.12.04.

[127] Page 90, in Letter Book from Nov.1875.

[128] Mary DUNCAN (1876- ?).

time, close to Nagpur, and Amelia would have been about 23. I searched in the OIOC and found her baptism record[129]:

> *'Amelia Barbara, baptised 9th January 1853, born 16th March 1852, daughter of George and Mary DUNCAN, abode: Seetabuldee, father's occupation: Conductor of Ordnance Dept.; Alfred WINLOCK (?), Chaplain, solemnised at Seetabuldee'.*

Amelia was only 3 ½ years old when her mother died, and was probably brought up by her stepmother Alice DUNCAN (née WILSON). We know she was alive in 1889 because she is mentioned (as *'Mrs A. Eagles'*) in her father's death notice of that year[130], living at Shillong, Assam.

I discovered in April 2003 that she married (before 1882) Thomas Cazaly EAGLES (c.1850s–aft.1905), who was Chief Superintendent of the Financial Department in Shillong, Assam. I have not yet been able to find a marriage record.

Note that a Thomas Henry EAGLES was instructor in Geometrical Drawing, Estimating & Architecture at the Royal India Engineering College, Coopers Hill, in 1872-92. If Thomas Cazaly Eagles was born c.1850, i.e. about the same time as his wife Amelia, then Thomas Henry might be a cousin, or not related. Did Thomas and Amelia die in India? If so, they might have left wills.

Amelia and Thomas had at least three children. Note that there were no more EAGLES baptisms in Bengal up to 1896.

    a. <u>Mary Alison EAGLES</u> [1/2] (c.1882-aft.1902) was born in about 1882, judging by her marriage record (see below).

    She married, on 22 December 1902 at Calcutta, an indigo planter named Cuthbert Henry GORDON (b.c.1872), son of William Ebenezer Gordon, and brother of her uncle William Robert Patrick Gordon[131]:

> *'Certificate of marriage: Calcutta; 22 Dec. 1902; Mary Alison EAGLES; age: 20; spinster; abode: Calcutta; father: Thomas Cazaly Eagles; Cuthbert Henry GORDON; age: 30; Indigo Planter; abode: Calcutta; father: William Ebenezer Gordon; married in the London Mission Chapel, Hastings, Calcutta, by me, A. Willifer Young, Minister of Religion,* [followed by original signatures of bride and groom], *witnesses: C.B. Harrison, H.E. Major'.*

Note that the family moved to Shillong (Bengal) from 1886, so baptisms were probably in that Presidency.

    b. <u>Nora Kathleen EAGLES</u> [1/2] (1886- ?) was born on 10 January 1886 and baptised at Shillong[132]:

---

[129] OIOC (N/2/32/30).

[130] OIOC (L/AG/34/14A/271).

[131] OIOC (N/11/10/572).

[132] OIOC (N/1/195/43).

'Baptisms solemnized at All Saints Church, Shillong, 1886: 1886 March 23, born: 1886 Jany 10; Nora Kathleen, daughter of Thomas Cazaly and Aurelia [sic] Barbara EAGLES; abode: Shillong; Chief Superintendent, Financial Dept.; H. Coleridge Spring, Chaplain'.

c. <u>Effie Jane EAGLES</u> [1/2] (1888-aft.1918) was born on 25 February 1888 and baptised at Shillong[133]:

'Baptisms solemnized at Shillong, 1888: 1888 May 1ˢᵗ, born: 1888 Feby 25ᵗʰ; Effie Jane, Daughter of Thomas Cazaly & Amelia Barbara EAGLES; abode: Shillong; Chief Superintendent Financial Dept.; Walter A. Hamilton, Chaplain'.

Effie married, on 25 November 1918, at Motihari, an indigo planter named James Fountain OWEN (c.1891-aft.1935), son of Edward Charles Gerard Owen[134]:

'Marriages solemnized at Motihari: 1918 November 25; James Fountain OWEN; 27; Bachelor; Indigo planter, Jagdispore, Mairshan, Saran; father: Edward Charles Gerard Owen; and Effie Jane EAGLES; 30; Spinster; abode: Motihari; father: Thomas Cazaley [sic] Eagles; by Licence; witnesses: G.S. Owen, J.C. Eagles [brother or sister of the bride?], M.A. Gordon [the bride's sister, Mary Alison née EAGLES], W.B. Heycock, M. Heycock; W.J. Simmons, Chaplain of Tirhoot & Champaran'.

Who is 'J.C. Eagles'? Might it be a brother or unmarried sister of Effie? The Heycocks might be related by marriage.

I traced James Owen's movements in Thacker's Directory, which showed the following:
1920   'asst Chuckia ind.con. P.O. Mairwa, Saran'.
1925   'asst Pursa, P.O. Lauriya, Champaran'.
1930   'asst Pursa, P.O. Lauriya, Champaran'.
1934   'asst Pursa, P.O. Lauriya, Champaran'.
1935   'asst Pursa, P.O. Lauriya, Champaran'.
1936   no entry.

A possible child is <u>Hilda Lilian OWEN</u> who married Captain John McGHIE on 5 December 1940 at Rawalpindi:

'Marriages solemnized at Rawalpindi (Church of Scotland): 1940 Decr. 5ᵗʰ; John McGHIE; age: major; Bachelor; Captain, R.A.M.C., abode: Rawalpindi; father: Henry McGhie; Hilda Lilian OWEN; age: major[i.e. born before 1919]; spinster; Q.A.I.M.N.S.; abode: Rawalpindi; father: James Owen; by Banns; witnesses: Nancy May Davies, William Lawrie[?]; Robert McC....Paterson, Acting Chaplain, Church of Scotland, Rawalpindi'.

---

[133] OIOC (N/1/204/36).
[134] OIOC (N/1/433/77).

We know that Effie OWEN (née EAGLES) settled in Cornwall, England, because in my paternal grandmother's address book, which had earlier entries by her sister Pearl, there are entries as follows:

> 'OWEN, Effie – Houston's cousin, a Dinwiddie'
>
> 'OWEN, Effie – Llandividly Cottage, Polperro Hooe, Cornwall (H's cousin)'

Although Effie OWEN was a cousin of my grandfather Houston DUNCAN, she was of course not a Dinwiddie!

7. **George Roan DUNCAN II** (1853-1901), my great-grandfather (see below), married **Mary Jane DINWIDDIE** (1848-1920).

8. Mary Faith DUNCAN [GGA] (1855-1897) was born on 18 July 1855, only about a month before her mother died and baptised at Sitabuldi, near Nagpur. The baptism record[135] states:

> 'Mary Faith, baptised 11 November 1855, born 18 July 1855, daughter of George Roan and Mary DUNCAN, abode: Seetabuldee; occupation: Dep.Asst. Commissary of Ordnance in the Nagpore Irregular Force; Alfred Kin…, Chaplain'.

She married George DE LA HOYDE [2/3] (1851-1917) at Sitabuldi, near Nagpur on 20 July 1875. The event was mentioned in a letter[136] from David Dinwiddie: *"Last month my Wife's eldest son George Delahoyde ventured down from the hills, Dalhousie, and got spliced to the youngest daughter of Captain Duncan, so our families are now doubly joined"*. This shows that George was the stepson of David Dinwiddie.

The marriage record[137] states:

> 'George De la HOYDE; age 24; bachelor; accountant PWD; father's name Christopher De La HOYDE; 20 July 1875 at All Saints Church, Seetabuldee; Mary Faith DUNCAN; age 20; spinster, father's name George Roan Duncan; witnesses: Lydia Duncan, George Roan Duncan, Thomas D. Dinwiddie.

I presume that the witness 'Lydia' was Mary's sister, and that 'Thomas D.Dinwiddie' was her sister-in-law's brother, i.e. Mary Jane Dinwiddie's brother Thomas David DINWIDDIE (1853-1904).

Mary died in Nagpur on 1 September 1897. The burial record[138] states:

> 'Burials at Nagpur: Church of England, Central Provinces; 1897 September 1; Mary Faith de la HOYDE; age: 42; wife of George de la Hoyde; buried: 1897 September 2; cause: Hepatitis disease (dropsy); C.H. Barlow, Chaplain'.

---

[135] OIOC (N/2/35/178).

[136] David Dinwiddie to General Blake, 30 Aug.1875.

[137] OIOC (N/1/153/152).

[138] OIOC (N/1/260/176).

This couple had at least nine children, listed here in summary:

a. <u>Mary Faith Olivia DE LA HOYDE</u> [1/2] (1877-aft.1912) was born on 10 May 1877 at Dalhousie, Punjab. She married William THIPTHORPE, and had at least three children.

b. <u>Hugh Duncan DE LA HOYDE</u> [1/2] (1879-1914) was born at Dalhousie, Bengal, on 23 January 1879. He is thought to have died unmarried and without issue.

c. <u>Emily DE LA HOYDE</u> [1/2] (1880- ?), known as 'Amy', was born on 10 October 1880 at Dalhousie, Punjab. She did not marry and retired to Newton Abbot, Devon.

d. <u>Bridget Lydia DE LA HOYDE</u> [1/2] (1882- ?) was born on 9 December 1882. 'Discovered' by me, she may have died in infancy.

e. <u>Alice DE LA HOYDE</u> [1/2] (1889- ?) was born on 25 March 1889. 'Discovered' by me, she may have died in infancy.

f. <u>Christopher Read Duncan DE LA HOYDE III</u> [1/2] (1890- ?) was born on 16 June 1890 at Sitabuldi, near Nagpur. He married (1st) Irene MacLEAN, who was born in Nairobi, Kenya, then married (2nd) Vida HUNTLEY and had seven children.

g. <u>George DE LA HOYDE II</u> [1/2] married Dorothy EDWARDS, and had three children.

h. <u>Freda DE LA HOYDE</u> [1/2] (? -1960), about whom we have no more information.

i. <u>Millicent Dorothy DE LA HOYDE</u> [1/2] (c.1896-1932) married a Mr PHILLIPPE, and had a son.

Details about the children and their descendants are in the chapter: The Thipthorps and De La Hoydes.

Marriage No.3: of **George Roan DUNCAN I** was to a Scottish spinster, 30 years younger than the groom, named Alice WILSON (c.1827-aft.1879), daughter of George Wilson, on 5 March 1858 at Sitabuldi, near Nagpur. The marriage record[139] states:

> '5th March 1858; George Roan DUNCAN, 61, widower; .....Commissary of Ordnance; abode: Seetabuldee; Father's name: William Duncan; Alice WILSON, 31, spinster; father's name: George Wilson; married by licence; witnesses: J.(or I). Knowles, M. Laville, F.J. Laville; H. Pigot James, Chaplain'.

The 'Laville' witnesses were almost certainly Maria LAVILLE (née PASLEY), and Francis James LAVILLE. Note that George Roan Duncan's age in this marriage record would make his birth year 1796/97.

David Dinwiddie wrote[140]: *"She is a Scotch woman from Lauder, a big town in Berwickshire"*. Also: *"He has been twice a widower, his present or third wife is a Scotch Lassie some 26 years younger than himself*[141]. *He picked her up in Kamptee, when she was in service with some officer's lady'*. She was actually 30 years younger.

David Dinwiddie also wrote: *"...his <u>third</u> wife, a Scotch Lass from Lauder, she came out to this country as Ladies Maid, about the time of the Mutiny and got wooed & married and all to Lt. Duncan, and has been, and still is a guide wife to the auld man. We always call him Captain Duncan. Mrs Duncan must be over 55 years, and she had two sons by Captain Duncan, both alive. Educated for some years at a school near Dollar..."*[142].

Thus we know a fair amount about the third wife. She was probably born in or near Lauder, of a quite humble family, since she was a maid. She came to India in the mid-1850s, and her employer was an officer in a regiment based in Kamthi in 1857/58. Alice evidently went from India to Limerick, Ireland in about 1867, judging by the letter from Robert DUNCAN (Appendix B): *'...we are all delighted beyond measure to hear that Mrs Duncan intends to come to this country very soon'*. It seems likely that she took Robert's daughter Thomasina out to India for the marriage to Alice's stepson William DUNCAN in February 1868.

Alice is not mentioned in the administration of her husband's will, and therefore might not have survived him, though she would have been only about 62 when her husband died. She is not recorded as 'Alice Duncan' in the 1891 or 1901 Censuses. Her baptism is not recorded in the Scottish Old Parish Records (1820-1840).

Note that when George married Alice, he had eight children from his 2nd marriage (to Mary Pasley, nee Leech). They were as follows, with ages in 1858:

Eliza DUNCAN	17
William George DUNCAN	14
Mary Laura DUNCAN	10
Robert Roan DUNCAN	9
Lydia Rebecca DUNCAN	8

---

[139] OIOC Index of Madras marriages (N/2/39/31).

[140] Letter No.44, 13-28 May 1879.

[141] Therefore born about 1825.

[142] DD letter to his sisters 10-26 Dec. 1877.

Amelia Barbara DUNCAN	6
George Roan DUNCAN	5
Mary Faith DUNCAN	3

George Roan DUNCAN and Alice WILSON had at least two children of their own. David DINWIDDIE wrote in 1879[143]: *"This Scotch wife has not been idle, so the upshot of the marriage is 2 fine young sons, one 12 and the other 14 years old!!! Both are now at a good school in a place called Dollar, not far from Edinburgh, where some of Mrs Duncan's friends are residing."*

When I first tried to trace the names and parentage of the boys from Dollar Academy records, the Archivist (Bruce Baillie) wrote to me on 26 April 2000 to give me a list of DUNCANs at the school at that time: *"Regret information very scanty but a John G. DUNCAN and a Henry L. DUNCAN are recorded as paying scholars in 1873-1876. An Arthur DUNCAN recorded 1876, a William DUNCAN 1876-1879 and a Thomas DUNCAN 1881-1882. John G. and Henry L. are several times recorded together, suggesting they were brothers"*. It turned out he was right in his suggestion!

'John' and 'Henry' are certainly not family names. But old George had had nine children already, so perhaps he decided his young wife should make the choices!

9. <u>John Gillespie DUNCAN</u> [GGU] (1861-bef.1933) was baptised in Madras, and the record[144] shows:

> *'John Gillespie, born 8 February 1861, baptised 24 March 1861 in Madras; father: George Roan DUNCAN; occ: Lt., and Dep. Asst., Commis. Ord.; abode: Sitabuldee, Nagpur'.*

In the 1901 Census his place of birth is given as 'Scotland', which would mean that his mother, and possibly his father, returned to Scotland in 1860.

The second name 'Gillespie' is interesting and is possibly Alice WILSON's maiden name or mother's maiden name. It might also be in honour of Colonel Gillespie, the hero of Vellore (ca.1807), and known as 'the bravest man in India'.

John married in West Ham, England in January-March 1895[145], to Selina Maud BOLITHO (c.1873-aft.1933), who was born in Parr(?), Cornwall[146], daughter of Richard Bolitho, mariner[147].

In his son's birth record (see below) John Gillespie Duncan is described as 'ship's rigger'. In the 1901 Census his occupation is 'Able Seaman', suggesting that he was in the merchant navy.

The couple were living in Thackeray Road, East Ham, Essex, at the time of the 1901 Census, though the house number is not clear; they are listed between 31 and 33 Thackeray

---

[143] Letter No.44, 13-28 May 1879.

[144] OIOC (N/2/42/54).

[145] Rootsweb Free BMDs (1895, Mar.; 4a, 2) and son's birth certificate.

[146] 1901 Census.

[147] Selina's 2nd marriage record.

Road, whereas they were at No.23 when their son George was born in 1903. The house location may lead to further clues about this family, and further children. Thackeray Road is between Barking Road and the East Ham and Barking By-pass; the nearest Underground Station is Upton Park on the District Line. Without having been there, I imagine Thackeray Road consists of terraced Victorian houses, designed for working class families.

In the 1901 Census, the family had a boarder, Richard BOLITHO, aged 38, born in Mullion, Cornwall, a 'Dock Labourer', who may have been an elder brother of Selina.

We know that John Gillespie DUNCAN died before 1933, because Selina Maud DUNCAN married on 30 December 1933 at the Registry Office, West Ham, aged 60, a widow, to John James GARVIE, aged 53, a mariner, of 30 Kingsland Road, Plaistow. The witnesses were M.J. Sharp, and T(?).A. Harrison.

I have so far discovered four sons and two daughters of John Gillespie DUNCAN and Selina, and there may be more. Three of the six known children died in infancy. The 1901 Census recorded the first four children, but not their second names. The official birth records (sourced in the Oxford Library) give second names, and at least two more children, born since 1901:

    a. Richard Ashton DUNCAN [1/2] (1896-1902) was born in Jan.-March 1896 in West Ham, London, and is recorded in the 1901 Census. He died, aged 6[148].

    b. James Bolitho DUNCAN [1/2] (1898-aft.1901) was born in Apr.-June 1898 in East Ham, probably in Thackeray Road, and is recorded in the 1901 Census.

    c. Dorothy Selina DUNCAN [1/2] (1899-1901) was born in July-Sept. 1899 in East Ham, probably in Thackeray Road, and is recorded in the 1901 Census. She died, aged 2 years[149].

    d. Rhoda DUNCAN [1/2] (1900-1901) was born in Oct.-Dec. 1900 in East Ham, probably in Thackeray Road, and is recorded in the 1901 Census. She died in infancy at about the same time as her sister Dorothy[150].

    e. George Roan DUNCAN IV [1/2] (1901- ?) was born on 1 November 1901 at 23 Thackeray Road, East Ham[151]:

> *'Registration District: West Ham; Sub-District: East Ham, Essex: First November 1901; 23 Thackeray Road, East Ham; George Roan; boy; father: John Gillispie [sic] DUNCAN; mother: Selina Maud DUNCAN formerly BOLITHO; occ.: Ship's Rigger; informant: S.M. Duncan, Mother, 23 Thackeray Road, East Ham; reg.: Thirteenth December 1901; Dan Reardon, Registrar'.*

---

[148] Free BMDs, W.Ham, Dec.1902 (4a, 142).

[149] Free BMDs, W.Ham, Sep.1901 (4a, 164).

[150] Free BMDs, W.Ham, Sep.1901 (4a, 154).

[151] GRO: BXBZ 581320.

Note that the 'George R. DUNCAN' who married Edith KETTLEY in Thornaby, Middlesborough District , on 26 September 1929[152] is not ours, based on the certificate. He was the son of Charles Watt Duncan.

f. John Gillespie DUNCAN II [1/2] (1903- ?) was born in Oct.-Dec. 1903 in West Ham, the registration district for East Ham, Essex. I have found no marriage or death record in Free BMDs.

Possible additional children were[153]:

DUNCAN, Gideon Alexander	June 1905	W.Ham 4a	127
DUNCAN, Gladys Brenda	Sept. 1905	W.Ham 4a	418
DUNCAN, James Walter	Dec, 1905	W.Ham 4a	293
DUNCAN, William Peter	Sept. 1906	W.Ham 4a	64

10. Henry Lauder DUNCAN [GGU] (1862-1931) was born on 1 June 1862, and baptised at Kamthi, near Nagpur. I found his baptismal record[154] at OIOC in April 2001.

> *'Henry Lauder, baptised 13 July 1862, born 1 June 1862, son of George Roan and Alison [sic] DUNCAN; abode: Sitabuldee; occupation: Lieutenant & Dep.Asst. Commissary of Ordnance; L. Hislop, Chaplain'.*

Henry's second name was probably in honour of the home town of his mother Alice/Alison WILSON. He returned to India after schooling in Scotland, joined the Postal Department (son's baptismal record), and became Deputy Postmaster General of the Indian Post and Telegraph Department.

He died on 9 September 1931 at Shillong, Assam[155]:

> *'Report of death of Mr H.L. Duncan, retired Deputy Postmaster General of the Indian Post & Telegraph Dept.; place of death: No.2 Cantonment, Shillong, Assam; cause: heart failure; age: 69 Y, 3M, 9D; wife: Mrs K.F. Duncan; sons: Capt. A.W. Duncan, 2/8th Gurkha Rifles, Shillong, Capt. D.L. Duncan, 1/8th Gurkha Rifles, Loralai'.*

He married Kathleen Florence DILLON (c.1863/64-1935), daughter of Luke Dillon, in Sitabuldi (near Nagpur) in 1885. Kathleen had a brother, Percival Richard Cecil DILLON, a barrister at Jabalpur, who married (10 August 1898, at Jabalpur) Ruth Susan ANDERSON, 2nd daughter of K.M. Anderson, of Jabalpur[156].

Note that a Luke DILLON (c.1759-1821) who died on 27 January 1821 was the brother of Lord Clonbrock.

The marriage record[157] of Henry and Kathleen states:

---

[152] GRO marriage records, sourced in Oxford Library.

[153] Free BMDs.

[154] OIOC (N/2/43/232).

[155] OIOC (L/AG/34/14A/15/265).

[156] 'The Friend of India', 25 August 1898.

[157] OIOC (N/1/191/152).

'Marriages solemnized at All Saints Church, Sitabuldi: 1885 Jan. 7th; Henry Lauder DUNCAN; age: 22; Bac.; Postal Dept., Nagpur; father: George Roan Duncan; Kathleen Florence DILLON; age: 21; Spins.; abode: Nagpur; father: Luke Dillon[158]; married by licence; witnesses: G.R. Duncan [groom's father], F.W. Dillon [bride's mother?]; G.F. Dennis, Chaplain'.

Kathleen died at Shillong aged 72 on 20 July 1935. The burial record[159] states:

'Return of burials at Shillong Cemetery: 1935 July 20, Kathleen Florence DUNCAN, 72, widow, buried: 1935 July 20; cause of death: gastro-enteritis; Walter Boulton, Chaplain of Shillong'.

Henry and Kathleen had at least three children, all sons. It is strange that they are 'spaced' so far apart – 1887, 1892, 1896. I've searched for 'missing' children to no avail. Note that Henry's death record mentions only the later two sons, Alan and Donald, suggesting that Harry died before 1931. Harry might have married and had children, e.g. if he died in 1930 he would have been 43. Alan had only one daughter, who left no descendants, and Donald appears not to have married. There may be no living descendants in this branch of the Duncan family.

a. Harry Dillon DUNCAN [1/2] (1887- ?) was born on 27 September 1887, and baptised at Sitabuldi, Nagpur. He was probably the first son, judging by his first and second names, though not certainly the first child. His baptismal record states:

'Baptisms solemnized at All Saints Church, Sitabuldi; 1887 Novr. 22nd; born: 1887 Septr. 27th; Harry Dillon, son of Harry Lauder and Kathleen Florence DUNCAN; res: Nagpur; father's occupation: Indian Postal Department; F.D. Gray, Chaplain'.

Harry is not mentioned in his father's death record of 1931, and may have died in infancy.

A Harry DUNCAN (no middle name) married in the Sheffield district in the March 1910 quarter[160], but there is only a slight chance this is the same person.

b. Alan Wilson DUNCAN [1/2] (1892-bef.1962) was born on 19 September 1892, and baptised at Sitabuldi. 'Alan' is not a family name, but 'Wilson' honours his paternal grandmother's family. There is a copy of his baptism certificate in his military record file at the British Library[161]:

'Baptisms solemnized at All Saints Church, Sitabuldi, Nagpur: 1892 Octr. 18; born: 1892 Sept. 19th; Alan Wilson, son of Henry Lauder & Kathleen DUNCAN; abode: Nagpur; Superintendent Govt Post Office Dept.; Arthur Charles Pearson, MA, Chaplain'.

---

[158] Of Allahabad, 'The Friend of India', 25 August 1898.

[159] OIOC (N/1/567/139).

[160] Free BMDs, Sheffield, Mar.1910 (9c, 668).

[161] OIOC (L/MIL/14/11410).

Alan was educated at St Paul's School in India, and Canterbury Agricultural College, Christchurch, NZ. He joined the NZ militia on 1.6.1910, and served in the NZ Expeditionary Force in 1914-1917 (2nd Lt. 5.5.15; Lt. 1.3.16). He was wounded at Gallipoli on 8 August 1915, and was mentioned in dispatches by Sir Douglas Haig while serving in France in 1916. He enlisted in the 2/8th Gurkha Rifles on 11.12.1917, and served with them until he retired in 1947 (Actg. Capt. 1.10.18, Capt. 1.4.20, Major 3.2.34, Lt.Col. 3.2.42, Col. 12.5.43). He was awarded the DSO for gallantry at Pandikkad, Malabar, during the Mapilla Rebellion of 1921-22. He also served in the Afghan Campaign of 1919/20, and Waziristan 1927. In 1946 he applied for permission to retire in England, with his wife and daughter; he was then Commandant of the 9th Gurkha Rifles Regimental Centre.

In April 2003 I phoned the Hon. Sec. of the 8th Gurkha Rifles Regimental Association (tel: 01608-676717), but he had no information about Duncan widows or children.

Alan married, on 16 June 1920, at Christchurch, New Zealand (Rev. Tobin, C of E), Joan Alice Isabel HAMBER (? –1962)[162], who was the 4th of nine siblings. Her birth was listed as Joan Alice Isabel HAMBER[163]. Her address was 423 Durham Street, Christchurch, NZ. Most of my information about the Duncan-Hamber connection, and this branch after 1946, comes from Dr George Hamber, a retired GP in Eastbourne[164].

Alan and Joan Duncan were living in the New Forest, Hampshire, probably in Milford-on-Sea, in 1946, when George Hamber visited them as a schoolboy.

Joan died on 19 September 1962, in the New Forest District[165], but was not buried in Brockenhurst. It is most probable that Alan also died in England.

Alan's military record lists as next of kin his uncle 'R. H. LANDOR, The Riddings [sic], Rugely', Staffordshire. He was Joan's uncle, probably Richard H. Landor, recorded in the 1901 Census as aged 40, a solicitor; his wife Ruth was Joan's aunt[166].

Alan and Joan had a daughter:

i) <u>Joyce Dillon DUNCAN</u> [2/1] (1921-2001) was born on 16 June 1921, and baptised at Lansdowne, Garwhal, India[167]. Note that Joyce's second name 'Dillon' honours her grandmother's family name. Her baptism record states:

'Baptisms solemnised at St Mary's, Lansdowne: 1921 July 30, 1921 June 16; Joyce Dillon, Daughter of Alan Wilson & Joan Alice

---

[162] Ibid.

[163] Sheet 6/8, #3880, presumably in NZ records.

[164] Dr George Hamber, 29 Vicarage Drive, Eastbourne, BN20 8AP (tel: 01323-725164) [georgehamber@yahoo.co.uk].

[165] GRO ref: New Forest, vol. 6b; folio 322 (from George Hamber).

[166] E-mail from Dr George Hamber (23.6.03) [georgehamber@yahoo.co.uk].

[167] OIOC (N/1/454/87).

DUNCAN; abode: Lansdowne; Capt. 2/8 Gurkha Rifles; G.A. Padfield, Chaplain'.

She attended St Monica's School, Kingsdown, Deal, Kent, in 1936, and probably returned to India before the War broke out. She went to England with her parents in 1946/47, then aged about 26, and probably unmarried. George Hamber remembers her as 'profoundly deaf'[168].

According to George Hamber (from letters) Joyce married John STEVENS (? –2003), also profoundly deaf. They had no children[169]. John died on 4(?) March 2003, while living in Christchurch, Hampshire.

Joyce Dillon STEVENS (née DUNCAN) died in England in 2001, aged about 80.

c. Donald Leslie DUNCAN $^{1/2}$ (1896-aft.1947) was born on 9 March 1896, at Rangoon[170]:

> *'C of E returns, Central Provinces: 1896 April 13th; born: 1896 March 9th; Donald Leslie, son of Henry Lauder and Kathleen Florence DUNCAN; abode: Rangoon; Sptdt. Of Post Office; Albert E. Brown, Constable, Chaplain, Nagpur'.*

He was first commissioned on 1.10.1915, in the 2/8th Gurkha Rifles, Cadet at Quetta 1916-17, 2nd Lt. 1.10.15, Lt. 1.10.16, Capt. 1.10.19, and attended the Australian Military College in 1920. He was 18 months in Mesopotamia with 2nd Gurkha Rifles, in the post 1st World War campaign, and joined the 1/8th Gurkha Rifles in 1923. He was promoted Brevet Major 1.7.33, Major 1.10.33, Act.Lt.Col. 1.10.40, Lt.Col. 7.12.40, T/Col. 18.8.45. He retired as Colonel Commandant, and proposed retiring to England.

His confidential reports list him as a keen shot and polo player, cheery, genial, and popular. He was promoted Major in 1934, 2 i.c. 8th Gurkhas in 1940, Lt.Col. 10.1941, Adm. Comd. Abbottabad 1943, Admin Commdt., Peshawar 1944, Actg. Col. 1945, Commdt. 8GRRC, Quetta. He served in Waziristan in 1938/39, and in Ceylon in 1942.

He listed as next of kin his father, and an aunt, Mrs W. YOUNG, 31 (later 84) Warrender Park Terrace, Edinburgh. This aunt might have been his father's sister, although we have no record of her. Alternatively, she might have been a married sister of Donald's mother Kathleen.

Donald was 51 years old when he presumably retired to England. It is conceivable that he married and had children there. The aunt's address in Edinburgh might be a clue for further research.

---

[168] E-mail from Dr George Hamber (22.6.03).

[169] ibid.

[170] OIOC (N/1/249/163).

I found no record of marriage or death in Free BMDs.

> Note: LIDDLE, Henry Lauder, b. Sept. 1893 Qr., Lanchester (10a, 364)
> LIDDLE, Henry Lauder, d. Dec. 1894 Qr., Lanchester (10a, 195)

Might be the son of a daughter of Henry and Kathleen DUNCAN.

Miscellaneous DUNCAN:

DUNCAN, George (b.c.1876), born in India, is recorded in the 1901 Census, living at 4 Charlton Green, Dover, Kent, England, with his wife Lavinia (b.c.1878), born in Sandgate, Kent.

CHAPTER 5: GEORGE ROAN DUNCAN II

GEORGE ROAN DUNCAN II (1853-1901), my great-grandfather, was born on 11 November 1853, at Kamthi or Sitabuldi. His father was based at the military cantonment of Kamthi during the early 1850s, but might have moved to Sitabuldi by 1853, where he would have been in charge of the cannons and powder.

Georges's birth date (on the baptism record below) can also be deduced from a letter written by his father-in-law, David DINWIDDIE on 4 September 1874: *"... the knot shall be tied on the 11th November next (DV) on the above date George Duncan will be of age...".*

Extract from ecclesiastical record of baptism of George Roan DUNCAN II (1853-1901)

The baptism record[171] states:

> 'Secunderabad, Shernagar, Seetabuldee, Trivandrum, Trichinopoly: George Roan, baptised 18th Dec.1853, born 11th Nov.1853, son of George and Mary DUNCAN; abode: Seetabuldee; occupation of father: Conductor of Ordnance Dept.; Alfred (surname illegible), Chaplain'.

---

[171] OIOC (N/2/32/312).

George Roan DUNCAN II (1853-1901)

We know surprisingly little about George Roan Duncan II - less than we know about his father. He seems to have trained as an accountant, and worked steadily for the Public Works Department, becoming Superintendent of the PWD Secretariat in Nagpur, probably quite an important position, as it was a huge government department at the time.

He married my great-grandmother, **Mary Jane DINWIDDIE** (1848-1918), known as 'Jane', on 23 December 1874, at Kamthi, near Nagpur, Bengal Presidency, India. He was just 21, and she was five years older than the groom, and had been engaged before. More information about Jane DINWIDDIE and her family is in my forthcoming book about THE DINWIDDIES. The marriage record[172] states:

> '*DUNCAN, George Roan; bachelor; of age; Accountant PWD, residing at Kamptee, father's name George Roan DUNCAN, 23 December 1874; Mary Jane DINWIDDIE; spinster; of age; father's name David DINWIDDIE; witnesses: M. E. Mills; W. Whatmore(?) Sergt. 44th Regt'.*

---

[172] OIOC (N/1/149/84).

Extract from ecclesiastical record showing marriage of George Roan DUNCAN II (1853-1901)
and Mary Jane DINWIDDIE (1848-1918)

Mary Jane DINWIDDIE (1848-1918)

Jane's father, David Dinwiddie wrote (1 January 1875): . *"My son in law George Duncan keeps the accounts at the D.P.W.* [Public Works Dept.] *on Rs 100 per mensem; he is a good and good looking young man, only 21 years of age...".* He was commissioned in the Nagpur Volunteer Rifles on 3 March 1886. I presume it is the uniform of this regiment that he is wearing in the photo below.

George Roan DUNCAN II (1853-1901)
with his son Houston George DUNCAN (1879-1961)

The following is a chronology of the life of George Roan DUNCAN II (1853-1901):

1853, Nov. 11   Born, probably in Kamthi or Nagpur.

1853, Dec. 18   Baptised at Sitabuldi, near Nagpur.

1874, Dec. 23   Married at Kamthi, near Nagpur, to Mary Jane DINWIDDIE, while Accountant, PWD.

1876, Oct. 31   Accountant, PWD, Kamthi (daughter Mary Emily's baptism).

1879, Mar 26   Accountant PWD (son Houston's baptism).

1880, Dec 2   Accountant, PWD (daughter Euphemia's baptism).

1882, June 14   Accountant, PWD, Kamthi (daughter Janet's baptism).

1883, Nov 29   Accountant, PWD, Kamthi (son David's baptism).

1884, Ayg. 7   Accountant, PWD, Kamthi (son David's burial).

1885, Mar 7   Accountant, PWD, Nagpur (son Thomas's burial).

1886, April 2   Superintendent, Chief Engineer's Office (son Thomas's burial).

1886, Nov 18   Superintendent, PWD Secretariat, Nagpur.

1900, Feb. 13 Government Pensioner, Nagpur (daughter Janet's burial).

1901, Oct 8 Died and buried, Nagpur (aged nearly 48).

Note that a George DUNCAN was at Cooper's Hill Engineering College and was destined for the Bombay Railways in 1877[173].

George and Jane evidently went to Wurrara (?) about 70-80 miles from Kamthi. *"Mr Duncan was obliged to go there for a few months, to keep accounts, but since Sept. last year he had been removed back again to Head Quarters offices at Nagpur"*[174]. In 1876 he was an Accountant 4th Grade in the PWD, Kanhan Division, having been appointed in that grade when he joined the Department on 23 November 1873[175]. By 1877 they were living in Kamthi: *"...now living in a nice little bungalow in this station doing duty in the PWD"*[176].

George Roan Duncan II died on 8 October 1901, aged 47 and 11 months, in Nagpur. His death record[177] states his age incorrectly: *'...aged 49; pensioner PWD; heptic abcess; buried Nagpur'*, i.e. he died of a liver abscess.

Extract from ecclesiastical record showing burial of George Roan DUNCAN II (1853-1901)

His widow, Mary Jane (nee DINWIDDIE) died in 1918. The burial record[178] states:

> *'Mary Jane DUNCAN, 72 years[179], relict of George Roan DUNCAN (PWD), buried on 8 December 1918 at General Episcopal Cemeteries, Lower ...Road & Park Street, Calcutta, died 4 December 1918, cause of death: cerebral apoplexy; F. Franklin, Chaplain of Kidderpore [a suburb of Calcutta]'.*

---

[173] L/PWD/8/13 (27 July 1877).
[174] David Dinwiddie to Margaret and Janet, 3 Jan.1876.
[175] OIOC (V/13/1073).
[176] David Dinwiddie to Gen. Blake, 27 Jan.1877.
[177] OIOC (N/1/296/126).
[178] OIOC (N/1/433/471).
[179] She was actually 70 when she died.

Extract from ecclesiastical record showing burial of Mary Jane DUNCAN (née DINWIDDIE) (1848-1918)

The couple had seven children, four sons and three daughters (but only eight grandchildren), listed here in summary, and then in detail:

1. Mary Emily DUNCAN (1876-1924) [GA] was born at Sitabuldi (near Nagpur) on 13 October 1876, and married Walter Gelston GILMORE (1860/1870-c.1934) in Nagpur on 20 January 1897. They had five children.

2. **George Houston DUNCAN** (1879-1961), OBE, my grandfather, known as 'Houston', was born on 10 February 1879 at Kamthi, near Nagpur, India. He married my grandmother, **Dulcie Cherry McKENNIE** (1885-1963), on 21 June 1905, at Bilaspur, Bengal, and died on 10 August 1961 at Zomba, Nyasaland (now Malawi). They had an only son, Richard, my father.

3. Euphemia DUNCAN [GA] (1880-aft.1950) was born at Raipur on 2 December 1880, and married, on 3 June 1908 at Kharagpur, David LESLIE (c.1874-aft.1947). They had two children.

4. Janet DUNCAN [GA] (1882-1900) was born at Kamthi, near Nagpur, on 12 May 1882, and died unmarried on 12 February 1900, buried at Nagpur.

5. David Dinwiddie DUNCAN [GU] (1883-1884) was born on 5 October 1883, baptised at Kamthi, and died in infancy at Kamthi on 7 August 1884.

6. Thomas Robert DUNCAN [GU] (1884-1886) was born on 7 December 1884, and baptised in Sitabuldi, Nagpur. He died in infancy at Sitabuldi, Nagpur, in 1886.

7. Alexander DUNCAN [GU] (1886-1943), CIE, known as 'Alec', was born on 3 October 1886, and baptised at Sitabuldi, Nagpur. He married on 23 May 1910, Pearl Marion McKENNIE [GA] (1887-1956), the younger sister of his brother Houston's wife, **Dulcie Cherry McKENNIE**, and died in Calcutta on 30 January 1943. They had no children.

Mary Jane DUNCAN (nee DINWIDDIE)(1848-1918),with two of her children, probably Mary Emily DUNCAN (1876-1924) & George Houston DUNCAN (1879-1961)

Here follow details of the children and their descendants:

1. <u>Mary Emily DUNCAN</u> (1876-1924) [GA] was born at Sitabuldi (near Nagpur) on 13 October 1876. The baptism record[180] states:

> *'Baptisms solemnized at All Saints Church, Sitabuldi: 1876 Oct. 31ˢᵗ; born: 1876 Oct.13ᵗʰ; Mary Emily DUNCAN; dr of George Roan and Mary Jane DUNCAN, abode: Kamthi; Accountant PWD; A.H. Etty(?), Chaplain'.*

I'm intrigued by her second name 'Emily' which was probably given in honour of Mary Jane DINWIDDIE's stepmother Emily (née HONEY), David DINWIDDIE's second wife.

Her grandfather David DINWIDDIE wrote:*" My daughter gave birth to a fine healthy girl on the 13ᵗʰ Oct. last, so I am a grandfather for the first time"[181]. As George and Jane were living near the Dinwiddies in Kamthi, David Dinwiddie mentions his granddaughter several times: "Your former correspondent Jane, has now a baby to care for, a fine plump healthy Daughter, now about 3 months old"[182]. "...Mrs Duncan with her guide man and little girl*

---

[180] OIOC (N/1/158/40).
[181] David Dinwiddie to Margaret and Janet, 3 Jan.1876.
[182] David Dinwiddie to Janet Fergusson, 27 Jan.1877.

Mary live close by our house here in Kamptee. I think I could walk to their bungalow in about 3 minutes. Their little Mary is now about 14 months old and toddling...".

Mary Emily DUNCAN (1876-1924),
Houston DUNCAN (1879-1961), and Janet DUNCAN(1882-1900)(?)

Mary married Walter Gelston GILMORE (1860/1870-c.1934) in Nagpur on 20 January 1897. He was the son of Denis Gilmore and Jane Bann. For more information about the GILMOREs, see THE GILMORE-FOSTER Family.

The marriage record[183] states:

> *'Marriages solemnized at All Saints Church, Nagpur; 1897 January 20; Walter Gelston GILMORE; age: full; Bachelor; Forest Department; abode: Bhandara(?); father: Charles Gilmore; Mary Emily DUNCAN, age: 20; Spinster; abode: Nagpur; father: George Roan Duncan; witnesses: R.. Dinwiddie, A. R. Hunt, G. Duncan; C. H. Barlow, Chaplain'.*

---

[183] OIOC (N/1/256/70).

'R.Dinwiddie' was Robert DINWIDDIE (1855-1922), the bride's uncle (with moustache, standing on the right in the wedding photo (below). 'A. R. Hunt' is, so far, not known. 'G. Duncan' was probably George Roan DUNCAN, the bride's father (on the bride's right in the wedding photo - below).

Wedding in 1897 of Mary Emily DUNCAN (1876-1924)
and Walter Gelston GILMORE (? –1934)

I think the lady seated near the bride in the wedding photo is Mary Jane DUNCAN (née DINWIDDIE), the bride's mother. The girl seated on Mary Jane's right could be 'Effie' DUNCAN (b.1880), the bride's younger sister.

Mary Emily was described by her son-in-law Esmond FOSTER thus (when writing for his children): *"She was very unfit and her heart was in a hopeless mess even then. She must have been a good-looking woman, but I never saw early photos of her. But by that time, eternal hot weathers, a large family, and inability to find money to go away for a change, had burnt out any beauty there may have been. I think it is very probable that the only time she left the plains of India was in 1914, when they took the children home to England and school." "... wonderfully sweet mother, who Mummy missed all her life".*

Mary GILMORE (née DUNCAN) took her children to England early in 1914, and they returned to India late in 1921. *"What the hot weather failed to destroy was her infinite kindness and sweetness, and that is why everyone wanted to talk to her by the hour. She had a very beautiful singing voice and was an able pianist. She had a low, rather husky, speaking voice, which was very attractive. In voice, there was a distinct resemblance between her and her younger brother Houston DUNCAN.". She died singing, with Mummy (Norah Estelle GILMORE) sitting beside her bed."*

Before she died, she and her husband Walter were building Gelston House, into which they intended to retire, but she died before it could be finished. Felicity FOSTER was born in Gelston House. Mary GILMORE (née DUNCAN) was buried beside her husband in Chhindwara cemetery, almost in sight of Gelston House.

Mary died on 22 May 1924 at Chhindwara. Her burial record[184] states:

> 'Burials at Chhindwara; 1924 May 22; Mary GILMORE; 47 years; Wife of Mr W.G. GILMORE, Deputy Conservator of Forests; buried: 1924 May 23rd; cause of death: Heart Failure; Aug. Furlong, Missionary'.

Mary and Walter had five children, and details of them and their descendants are in THE GILMORE-FOSTER FAMILY.

    a. <u>Oliver(?) GILMORE</u> [1/1] (1898-1900?) was born on 11 August 1898 at *'Wavangal, Nizam's Dominions',* and died of cholera at the age of two.

    b. <u>Eileen Gelston Duncan GILMORE</u> [1/1] (1900- ?) was born in India and married, at Raipur, India, on 26 January 1921, Herbert Jasper BELL (c.1887- ?), known as 'Jasper'. They had six children.

    c. <u>Norah Estelle GILMORE</u> [1/1] (1902-1959) was born on 30 June 1902, and baptised at Chhindwara. She married Esmond Lewis Pearce FOSTER on the 25 September 1926, and they had four children.

    d. <u>Kathleen GILMORE</u> [1/1] (1903- ?) known as 'Peggy', was born on 18 November 1903, and baptised on 31 December 1903. She married Vivian Terence CROLEY, known as 'Terence', at Asirgarh, in February 1929. They had one child, a son, Oliver CROLEY.

    e. <u>Walter Charles Gelston GILMORE</u> [1/1] (1908-1942), known as 'Charles', was born on 6 March 1908, and baptised on 18 June 1908 at Indore. He died on 9 April 1942 in Hong Kong, some four months after the island fell to the Japanese on Christmas Day 1941.

---

[184] OIOC (N/1/477/199).

2. **George Houston DUNCAN** (1879-1961), OBE, my grandfather, known as 'Houston', was born on 10 February 1879 at Kamthi, near Nagpur, India (for details, see the next chapter).

3. Euphemia DUNCAN [GA] (1880-aft.1950) was born at Raipur on 2 December 1880. Her birth record[185] shows:

> *'DUNCAN, Euphemia, b. 2 December 1880; dau.of George Rone [sic], occupation: accountant, and Mary Jane; abode: Raipur'.*

She married, on 3 June 1908 at Kharagpur, David LESLIE (c.1874-aft.1947), Deputy Chief Engineer of the Bengal Nagpur Railway. The marriage record[186] states:

> *'Marriages solemnised at Khargpur: 1908 June 3; David LESLIE, 34, Bachelor; District Engineer, B.N.R, Garden Reach; father: George Dunlop Leslie; and Euphemia DUNCAN, 27, Spinster; abode: Khargpur; father: George Roan Duncan; by Banns; witnesses: R. Dinwiddie [Bride's cousin], K.W. Digby, J.C. Tindel(?); Walter K. Firminger, Chaplain of Kidderpore'.*

Euphemia LESLIE (née DUNCAN) (1880-aft.1947)

---

[185] OIOC (N/1/175/51).
[186] OIOC (N/1/349/14).

And after 33 years service, David Leslie retired in 1928 to 'Edencourt', St John's Road, Bexhill, Sussex. When I was a schoolboy, I met Uncle David and Aunt Effie at Bexhill (c.1947). They had two children:

    a. <u>Barbara Celia LESLIE</u> [1/1] (1910-aft.1947) was born on 1 February 1910, and baptised at Nagpur. The baptism record states:

> *'Baptisms solemnised at All Saints Church, Nagpur: 1910 Feby.1ˢᵗ; Barbara Celia, female; parents: David and Euphemia LESLIE; abode: Nagpur; occ.: Engineer; Cyril Price, Asst. Chaplain'.*

Barbara suffered from *petit mal*, and did not marry, though she travelled independently after her parents died.

    b. <u>'Winkie' LESLIE</u> [1/1] was institutionalised with some kind of mental disorder. My mother says that he was the reason that Alex and Pearl Duncan were afraid to have children (see below).

4. <u>Janet DUNCAN</u> [GA] (1882-1900) was 'discovered' by me through her burial record. She was born on 12 May 1882 and baptised at Kamthi. Her baptism record[187] states:

> *'Baptisms solemnized at Kamptee: baptised: 1882 June 14; born: 1882 May 12ᵗʰ; Janet, Daughter of George and Mary Jane DUNCAN; abode: Kamptee; Accountant PWD; Robt. Langford, Chaplain'.*

She died on 12 February 1900 at Nagpur. I made an accidental discovery of her burial record[188] at the OIOC, British Library:

> *'Burials at Nagpur, C of E, Central Provinces, 12th Feb. 1900, Janet DUNCAN, aged 17, daughter of G.R. Duncan, Gov't. Pensioner, buried on 13ᵗʰ Feb. 1900, cause of death: intestinal obstruction; C.H. Barlow, Chaplain'.*

5. <u>David Dinwiddie DUNCAN</u> [GU] (1883-1884) was 'discovered' by me. He was born on 5 October 1883 and baptised at Kamthi. His baptism record[189] states:

> *'Baptisms solemnized at Kamptee: baptised: 1883 Nov. 29ᵗʰ; born: 1883 Oct. 5ᵗʰ; David Dinwiddie; male; son of George and Mary DUNCAN; abode: Kamptee; Accountant, PWD; J.O.F. Willcocks, Chaplain'.*

David died in infancy and was buried at Kamthi on 7 August 1884. The burial record[190] states:

---

[187] OIOC (N/1/180/28).
[188] OIOC (N/1/281/137f).
[189] OIOC (N/1/186/29).
[190] OIOC (N/1/189/96).

'Burial at Kamptee; 1884 August 7th; David Dinwiddie DUNCAN; age: 10 mths; son of G. Duncan, Accountant, PWD; buried: 1884 August 8th; cause of death: Remittent fever; J. O. F. Willcock, Chaplain'.

6. <u>Thomas Robert DUNCAN</u> ^{GU} (1884-1886) was 'discovered' by me in the OIOC records in March 2002. He was born on 7 December 1884. His birth fills a gap that existed between the births of David and Alexander. He was probably born in Kamthi or Nagpur, where he was baptised[191].

'Baptisms solemnized at All Saints Church, Sitabuldi: 1885 March 7th; born: 1884 Decr. 7th; Thomas Robert, son of George Roan and Mary DUNCAN; abode: Nagpur; occup.: Accountant, P.W.D.; G.F. Dennis, Chaplain'.

Thomas died in infancy. His burial record[192] states:

'Burials at Seetabuldee, Nagpur: 1886 April 2nd; Thomas Robert; age: 1 year and 4 months; infant son of George R. DUNCAN, Supt. Chief Engineer's Office; cause: Laryngitis; F.D. Gray, Chaplain'.

7. <u>Alexander DUNCAN</u> ^{GU} (1886-1943), CIE, known as 'Alec', was born in Sitabuldi (near Nagpur) on 3 October 1886. His baptism record[193] states:

'Baptisms solemnized at All Saints Church, Sitabuldi; 1886 Novr. 18th; born: 1886 October 3d; Alexander, son of George Roan and Mary Jane DUNCAN; residence: Nagpur; father's occupation: Superintendant P.W. [Public Works] Secretariat; F.D. Gray, Chaplain'. No sponsors were listed.

---

[191] OIOC (N/1/191/37).
[192] OIOC (N/1/196/236).
[193] OIOC (N/1/198/50).

Alexander DUNCAN (1886-1943)

He died on 30 January 1943, aged only 56. There is an entry about him in 'Who was Who'[194]: *'DUNCAN, Alexander, CIE (1941), Agent & General Manager, Bengal-Nagpur Railway Co., Calcutta, died 30 January 1943'.* The following obituary appeared in the February 1943 edition of the Bengal Nagpur Railway Magazine:

'MR ALEXANDER DUNCAN'S OUTSTANDING CAREER

MR DUNCAN was born on the 3rd October, 1886, and entered the service of the Bengal Nagpur Railway as long ago as the 16th March 1903. After undergoing preliminary training, initially in the duties of a Guard and subsequently in those of an Assistant Station Master and Traffic Inspector, Mr. Duncan was appointed as an Assistant Traffic Superintendent on the lst January, 1904. He first secured acting promotion as District Traffic Superintendent at Khurda Road on the 8th July 1908, and continued to officiate in this capacity from time to time during the years 1908 to 1914. In March 1912, he was transferred to the Agent's Office as 3rd Personal Assistant, being employed in this capacity up to the 5th January 1914, and again in the same post from the 9th November 1914, to the 21st February 1916, inclusive. After reverting to his substantive appointment as Assistant Traffic Superintendent (with effect from the 22nd February, 1916) he resigned this

---

[194] British Library, WwW 1941-50 (p.335).

last-mentioned post an the 15th September 1916, in order to take up a post with the firm of Messrs. Andrew Yule and Co.

Following his re-appointment to the Bengal Nagpur Railway service, Mr. Duncan reported for duty to the then General Traffic Manager on the lst November 1919, but during that month was posted as lst Personal Assistant to the Agent. With effect frorn the lst December 1919, he was again promoted to act as District Traffic Superintendent (this time at Nainpur). Mr. Duncan returned to the Agent's Office as 1st Personal Assistant on the 1st April 1920, and while holding this post was confirmed as District Traffic Superintendent with effect from the lst October 1920. He secured further promotion as acting Deputy Manager during the period March to May 1921, and, after reverting to the post of lst Personal Assistant to the Agent, his services were loaned to the Government of India as Assistant Secretary to the Railway Board, with effect from the 23rd July 1921. Mr. Duncan returned to the Bengal Nagpur Railway as District Traffic Superintendent at Headquarters on the lst February 1923, being subsequently posted to Adra and Khurda Road in the same capacity. On the 12th March 1925, he became Coal Manager at Adra and on the 1st May of the same year returned to the Agent's Office as Acting Deputy Manager.

On the 24th November 1925, Mr Duncan was appointed to act as Superintendent, Transportation, Traffic, and subsequently as Transportation Manager (with effect from the 6th March 1926). After officiating again as Superintendent, Transportation, Traffic, with effect from the 7th November 1926, Mr. Duncan was confirmed in the last-mentioned appointment on and from the lst April 1927. He was again promoted to act as Transportation Manager from the 6th November 1927, and, after reverting to his substantive post as Superintendent, Transportation, Traffic (in February 1928), he was transferred to the Agent's Office with the rank of Deputy Manager, with effect from the 16th November 1928. On the 1st November 1929, he secured permanent promotion as Transportation Manager of the Bengal Nagpur Railway and succeeded the late Sir Vivian Jarrad as Agent of the Railway, with effect from the 1st May 1937.

While holding the rank of Major in the B. N. Ry. Battalion, Auxiliary Force (India), Mr. Duncan was awarded the Officers' Volunteer Decoration on the 22nd October 1926. He subsequently commanded the Battalion with the rank of Lt.-Colonel, during the period lst April 1933, to 31st March 1938. On the 27th March 1934, he was appointed an Honorary Aide-de-Camp on the Personal Staff of His Excellency the Viceroy and Governor-General with the honorary rank of Colonel. Mr Duncan was selected for the award of the C. I. E. in the King Emperor's Birthday Honours List in June 1941, and was appointed Honorary Colonel of the B. N. Ry. Battalion A.F.(I) on the 29th July 1941.

Mr Duncan relieved Mr. C. A. Muirhead, C.I.E., Agent and General Manager, South Indian Railway, as President of the Indian Railway Conference Association during the period lst January to 31st March 1941 and was elected to hold the same office during the financial year 1941-42.

Following his appointment as Agent and General Manager of the Bengal Nagpur Railway, Mr. Duncan served as a Commissioner for the Port of Calcutta and as Administrative Officer, Vizagapatam Harbour'.

Alec Duncan married on 23 May 1910, perhaps at Kharagpur, <u>Pearl Marion McKENNIE</u> [GA] (1887-1956), the younger sister of his brother Houston's wife, **Dulcie Cherry McKENNIE**, my grandmother (see my book THE McKENNIE). They had no children. The marriage record[195] states:

> *'1910 May 23; Alexander DUNCAN, 23, Bachelor, D.T.S.*[District Traffic Superintendent], *B.N.R.* [Bengal Nagpur Railway], *Khargpur, father: George Roan Duncan (deceased); Pearl Marion McKENNIE, 21, Spinster; abode: Khargpur, father: Richard Cherry McKennie (deceased); married by banns; witnesses: N. S. Duncan, L. W. Carter, V.S. John Corby (or Croley); W.J. Simmons, Chaplain'.*

I wonder who the witness 'N. S. Duncan' was? Probably the wife of a Duncan male, or one of Henry Lauder Duncan's children (born 1885 ->).

---

[195] OIOC (N/1/365/15).

CHAPTER 6: GEORGE HOUSTON DUNCAN

George Houston DUNCAN (1879-1961), OBE, my grandfather, known as 'Houston', was born on 10 February 1879 at Kamthi, near Nagpur, India, and died on 10 August 1961 at Zomba, Nyasaland (now Malawi), aged 82. The name 'Houston' comes from his maternal great-grandmother, Susannah HOUSTON (see forthcoming THE DINWIDDIES), and was passed down as a second name to his son and grandson {Brian}.

Among memorabilia in my possession is a copy of the baptismal certificate:

> *'At Christ Church, Kamptee, diocese of Nagpur, on 26 March 1879, said to be born on 10 February 1879, George Houston, son of George and Jane DUNCAN, abode Kamptee, father's trade/profession: accountant, DPW [Public Works Dept.]; signed William H. GALE, Chaplain'.*

Extract from ecclesiastical record showing baptism of George Houston DUNCAN (1879-1961)

George Houston DUNCAN (1879-1961) known as 'Houston'
(at wedding of Thomas DINWIDDIE in 1886)

He joined the Bengal Nagpur Railway with a recommendation from his uncle, Robert DINWIDDIE (1855-1922), who was the Railway's Deputy Auditor. He enrolled in the Bengal Volunteer Rifles, and was part of the contingent from India at the coronation of King Edward VII in 1912.

Among memorabilia in my possession are:

a) Calcutta University entrance exam pass certificate, Jan. 1896, for G.H. DUNCAN.

b) Note written on 29 March 1897 by (illegible signature) says: *"Mr George DUNCAN is the son of a First Grade Accountant; his uncle Mr Robert DINWIDDIE is the Dy. Auditor of the B.N. Ry...".* *"DUNCAN is quite young about 20, he is of pure Scotch descent... stands about 6' or over... He has received a good education at one of the best schools at Darjeeling..."* (St.Paul's at Jalapahar).

c) A note from the Agent (signature illegible) dated 5 April 1897: *"I have known Mr G. H. DUNCAN and his family for the last ten years. His father was Superintendent of the PWD Secretariat .... CP. His grandfather was an officer of the Rd EI Co Service. His uncle is our Deputy Auditor"* [Robert Dinwiddie].

d) G. H. DUNCAN (with signature) applied for leave (to the Agent and Chief Engineer of BNR) on 20 September 1898, from Midnapur (Jherriah) Survey. G.H. DUNCAN appointed Sub-Divisional Officer 13 November 1898.

e) G.H. DUNCAN went to the Coronation of Edward VII in 1902, and one of the documents, describing him as Serg. G.H. DUNCAN is signed 'Houston DUNCAN'.

f) H.G. DUNCAN: programme of BNR Ry Rifles - Sports 1904 states Hon. Sec as 'Sergt. H.G. DUNCAN'.

g) G. H. DUNCAN appointed 2nd Lt. in Volunteer Services of India from 20 October 1906 (the year his son Richard was born). Lt. H.G. DUNCAN Bengal Vol. Rifles, 18 Feb.1910. G. H. DUNCAN, VD, appointed Captain in Indian Defence Force on 1 April 1917.

From the foregoing, I concluded that my grandfather was probably called 'Houston' by his family to avoid confusion with the two older George's, and then adopted the name in documents. The most compelling evidence comes from the Coronation document (1902), that refers to G.H. DUNCAN, but is signed 'Houston DUNCAN'.

George Houston DUNCAN (1879-1961) known as 'Houston', in 1925

Houston DUNCAN was created OBE on 3 June 1919. He left the Bengal Nagpur Railways (BNR) in about 1924[196] to become General Manager of Nyasaland Railways. He retired to Rath Drum Farm[197], Zomba in 1936. We do not know the origin of the name, but presumably it had some family connection with the town in Ireland. Houston was one of two non-official Members of the Legislative Council of Nyasaland, appointed by the Governor, the other members being Colonial Government officials.

---

[196] Based on his years of residence in Nyasaland at his death (see death certificate and note).

[197] 'Rath Drum' means 'fort on the hill'; there is a market town with that name in Co. Wicklow, 29 miles SW of Dublin.

He married my grandmother, **Dulcie Cherry McKENNIE** (1885-1963), on 21 June 1905, at Bilaspur, Bengal. The marriage record[198] (below) shows:

> 'At Bilaspur Civil Station; 1905 June 21; George Houston DUNCAN; 26; Bachelor; Acting D.T.S. [District Traffic Superintendant], B.N.Ry.; abode: Bilaspur; father: George Roan Duncan (deceased); and Dulcie Cherry McKENNIE; 20; Spinster; abode: Bilaspur; father: Richard Cherry McKennie (deceased); witnesses: J. W. Woods, M. J. Duncan [groom's mother], A. Duncan [groom's brother?], R. Dinwiddie [groom's uncle], E. Duncan [groom's sister]; Arthur F. G. Wardell, Chaplain of Chhattisgarh'.

Marriage record of George Houston DUNCAN & Dulcie Cherry McKENNIE

In her prayer book[199] Dulcie wrote: 'Dad and I were married from this prayer book by Mr Wardell in your Aunt Mary Gilmore's drawing room in Bilaspore & we went away in a smart black trap drawn by Gay Lass from the Civil Station to our own bungalow in Bilaspore'. The marriage took place only four months after Dulcie's father had died. There were no witnesses from her side of the family. For more information about her family, see the Chapter THE McKENNIES.

Houston died at Rath Drum Farm, Zomba, Nyasaland (now Malawi) on 10 August 1961; the death certificate states:

> 'No. 429/2637: 10th August 1961; 1.30 a.m.; Rathdrum Farm, Zomba; cause: Congestive Cardiac Failure; Houston George DUNCAN; abode: Rathdrum Farm, Zomba; occupation: farmer; nationality: British; male; age: 84 years; length of residence in the Protectorate: 36 years; Dilip Kumar Desai, Government Medical Officer, Zomba; date of registration: 13th September 1961; witnessed: Henry Granville Martin'.

Dulcie wrote against the age: 82, 6 m. (which is correct), and against the length of residence (in Malawi), 37.

The funeral service was conducted by the Revd. Shelburn, Church of Christ, Namikanga, Malawi on 10 August 1961 'when our own C of E Padre refused'[200].

---

[198] OIOC (N/1/324/306).

[199] In the possession of my sister Philippa.

[200] Dulcie Duncan's address book.

Dulcie died in Zomba, Nyasaland, on 13 November 1963, aged 78, and was buried at Rath Drum Farm with her husband and son (see below).

Houston and Dulcie DUNCAN had one child:

1. **<u>Richard Houston Roan DUNCAN</u>** (1906-1963), my father, was born on 22 May 1906 at Kharagpur, Bengal, India (see below).

Richard Houston Roan DUNCAN (1906-1963), my father, known as 'Dick', was born on 22 May 1906 at Kharagpur, Bengal, India. The baptism record[201] shows that he was baptised, probably in Kharagpur on 16 March 1907, i.e. about ten months after he was born:

> 'Baptised: 1907 March 16; born: 1906 May 22; Richard Houston Roan, son of Houston George and Dulcie Cherry DUNCAN; abode: Khargpur; father's occupation: District Traffic Superintendent B.N.R.; Cecil G. Stottar(?), Chaplain of Cuttack'.

Year.	Month.	Day.	Year.	Month.	Day.	Child's Christian Name.	Sex.	Christian.	Surname.	Abode of Parents.	Quality, Trade, or Profession of Father.	Na
1907	March	16	1906	May	22	Richard Houston Roan	Son of	Houston George + Dulcie Cherry	Duncan ✓	Khargpur	District Traffic Superintendent B.N.R.	Ces

Extract from ecclesiastical record showing baptism of Richard Houston Roan DUNCAN (1906-1963)

---

[201] OIOC (N/1/338/36).

<u>Richard Houston Roan DUNCAN (1906-1963) with his parents</u>

He was educated at Victoria College, Darjeeling, and Geelong Grammar School, Geelong, Victoria, Australia, then spent two years at Sydney Sussex College, Cambridge, studying mechanical engineering. He was Captain of Rowing at the College, and rowed in 'Goldie' the University 2nd VIII in 1926(?). He left Cambridge before graduating to join the Bengal Nagpur Railway.

Members of the Winning Crew, J. A. Hardy (stroke) is holding the Fairbairn Challenge Cup.

Members of the Geelong College crew that won the Head of River Race in 1924 (Richard Duncan on left)

The finish of the Head of River Race, 1924

He met my mother **Elisabeth BRACKEN,** known as 'Betty', at parties in Cheltenham in about 1925, when he was at Cambridge and she was at the Cheltenham Ladies College[202]. She was a pupil at the school from January 1920 to July 1926. They did not become formally engaged until she went back to India in about 1926. They married on 2 March 1928 at St. Paul's Church, Waltair, Madras Presidency[203], India, where her father was Collector in the Indian Civil Service.

Wedding of Richard Duncan and Elizabeth Bracken; with Jimmy Coode (best man), Catherine Bracken (bridesmaid), and Patricia Salt (flower girl)

---

[202] Recollections of Betty Duncan in 2002.

[203] Now in the State of Andhra Pradesh.

The marriage record[204] shows: *'Marriages solemnised at St Paul's Church, Waltair; 1929 March 2nd; Richard Houston Roan DUNCAN, 22, Bachelor, Railway Officer, abode: Adhra; father: Houston George Duncan; and Elisabeth BRACKEN, 20, Spinster, abode: Waltair; father: Geoffrey Thomas Hirst Bracken; by banns; witnesses: G.T.H. Bracken* [bride's father], *Houston George Duncan* [groom's father], *Beatrice Bracken* [bride's mother]; *George Albert Wilson, Chaplain'.*

Wedding of Richard Houston Roan DUNCAN (1906-1963) and Elizabeth BRACKEN (b.1908); Standing (l to r): Geoffrey Thomas Hirst BRACKEN (1879-1951)(bride's father);Jimmy Coode (best man); Groom; Houston DUNCAN (1879-1961)(groom's father); seated (l to r): Dulcie Cherry DUNCAN (nee McKENNIE)(1885-1963)(groom's mother); Catherine Philippa BRACKEN (1914-1998) (bride's sister); bride; Patricia Salt (flower girl); Beatrice Hastings BRACKEN (1878-1964)(bride's mother)

---

[204] OIOC (N/2/145/166).

A WALTAIR WEDDING

DUNCAN—BRACKEN.

(From a Correspondent)

Waltair, Mar. 2.

A gay cold weather in Waltair was brought to a close to-day by the wedding of Miss Betty Bracken, elder daughter of Mr. G. T. H. Bracken, I.C.S., and Mrs. Bracken, to Mr. Richard Houston Duncan, B. N. Railway, only son of Mr. and Mrs. H. G. Duncan.

St. Paul's Church which had been decorated by Mrs. Hodding and other kind helpers, with pink and white flowers and ferns, looked beautiful. The bride arrived punctually at 9 o'clock, and came up the aisle on her father's arm, preceded by a choir of boys from St. John's Church, Vizagapatam to the strains of "Lead us Heavenly Father, Lead us", beautifully rendered on the organ by Mr. W. Macmillan.

The young bride looked charming in a Juliet dress of white ring velvet (by Maude Uidler). The long dipping skirt was lined with palest rose pink, and embroidered in silver and pearls to match the neck and wrists, while the note of pale pink was repeated in the graceful tulle veil and train, which fell from a Juliet cap of pearls and orange blossom. She carried a small prayer book, bound in white and silver, and a pair of silver shoes completed the attractive picture.

Patricia Salt made a sweet little flower girl in a mediaeval frock of pale pink charmeuse trimmed with swan'sdown, a wreath of pink rosebuds crowned her golden curls and as she preceded the bride up the aisle

she scattered rose petals from a silver basket.

Miss Catherine Bracken, younger sister of the bride, looked most attractive in a dress of soft blue ninon with a fluttering skirt and sleeves. She wore a large blue crinoline hat to match, and carried a bouquet of pink and white roses.

The mother of the bride wore a becoming gown of love-in-the-mist grey georgette embossed with turquoise blue flowers, with a blue hat to match. She carried a sheaf of cornflowers.

The bridegroom's mother wore a graceful georgette gown patterned with pink roses on a black ground; she wore a smart black hat.

Mr. James Coode was best man, and Messrs. Bell, Donald, Greenham and Muir were ushers.

After the ceremony and the signing of the register all the guests adjourned to the Club where they were received by the bride and bridegroom, and the wedding breakfast was served. Directly after breakfast, at Mr. and Mrs. Bracken's invitation everyone went to the Collector's Bungalow, where the Wedding Cake was cut under a large horseshoe. The health of the bride was proposed in a humorous speech by Mr. Charles Hodding. The bridegroom then responded in a short speech, and finally proposed the health of the bridesmaids, to which Mr. Coode replied.

Mr. and Mrs. Duncan left by car amid a shower of confetti, for Vizianagram to catch the mail for the North. The bride's going away dress was a three piece costume of sky blue crepe-de-chine, with a grey and blue patterned waistcoat, and a grey straw hat to match.

Mr. Richard Houston Duncan was at Sidney Sussex College, Cambridge, where he captained his college boat crew, and rowed at Henley. Since coming to India he has played hockey and football with signal success, and is a member of his Railway football team. Like his bride, he is very keen on riding.

Miss Betty Bracken came out East in November, 1927, to Cocanada. Since then she has spent the hot weather hunting in Ootacamund, where she came in second in the Ladies Point-to-Point. She will be much missed in Waltair, where she has organised many amusing parties.

All their friends combined to wish them many years of happiness and prosperity.

For more information about Elisabeth BRACKEN see my forthcoming book about HIRST and BRACKEN.

I don't know why my father left Cambridge before graduating. I heard, perhaps from him, or my grandparents, or my mother, that he was advised to join the BNR quickly, to get ahead of a cohort of other recruits. I know he wished he could have spent another year at university, if only to have had a chance to get into the Cambridge crew for the Boat Race.

My father worked his way up 'through the ranks' in the BNR, although it must have helped that his uncle was in the top echelon of the company, finally become Agent (CEO). I regret that I do not know where he was posted during his career. It should be possible to construct the process from the letters my mother wrote to her mother, many of which are in the possession of my sister Philippa. More information may be found in her contributions to Encycloparent, a 'round-robin' for women scattered round the global that she belonged to from the time we were born until the 1950s.

The main locations I remember were: Waltair (a suburb of the port Vizagapatam), Adra, and Khargpur. The latter was the mechanical headquarters of the BNR, as distinct from the administrative headquarters in Calcutta. It was where my father and I were born, and its main claims to fame are: a) that it has the longest railway station platform in the world, and b) it is the site of the Asian Institute of Technology.

My father served in the army reserve before WW2, possibly starting in the BNR battalion, but mostly in the 1/18th Royal Garwhal Rifles. He served with the regiment in the NW Frontier Province (now in Pakistan), when we lived in Campbellpur. He also spent time in Lansdowne, the regimental HQ in the foothills of the Himalayas.

At some time he learned to fly, encouraged by Colonel Arthur Martin-Leake, the Chief Medical Officer of the BNR, who had the distinction of being one of only three recipients of a bar to the Victoria Cross. His were both awarded for tending to wounded soldiers while under fire, the first in the Boer War, and the second in WW1. It was he who removed my adenoids. Wikipedia says he retired to England in 1937. My mother also got her pilots licence.

When WW2 started my father was in a 'reserved occupation' because the Indian railways were so important in the process of moving men and materials, initially to Africa and Europe, and later to the China-Burma-India (CBI) theatre. We know most about his service in a Force 136 expedition to the Andaman Islands through an account written by my godfather Terence Croley, who commanded the expedition. Terence was married to Peggy, my father's cousin. The following extract from his story tells us a bit about the circumstances:

"Dick and I were both from the same Indian railway[205]. When the war started, he went to the Garwhalis[206] and to Burma, and I went to an Indian cavalry regiment and Eritrea and Egypt. We were both recalled to raise Sapper companies in 1942. In 1943 I wangled this job, and Dick took over my company. A week before we sailed, one of my officers went sick, and I heard that Dick had been ordered back to civil employment. After a quick signal to Delhi, he was allotted to me. We lived in dread, waiting for the axe to fall, as I had gone over everyone's heads in my signal. Half an hour before we sailed, a signal was brought to Captain 'S' on the depot ship - "Under no circumstances is Major Duncan to sail on sortie." Captain 'S' gave it to me and I said, "Can you help?" He wrote across the

---

[205] See Appendix A: Biographical Notes.
[206] 8th Royal Garwhal Rifles.

signal, *"Your message not understood. Repeat"*, *and handed it to the messenger. We sailed. Four hours later a similar message arrived stating that if we sailed Dick was not to land, but to return at the conclusion of the submarine sortie. I'm afraid we just didn't do anything about that.*

From the above account we know that my father served in Burma. I do not know in what capacity, but I suspect that he might have advised on transport matters connected with the Burma Road that ran from India to China. I never heard him talk about it. I doubt that he had any involvement with the Chindits, because I think we would have heard about it.

Richard Duncan became Traffic Manager before taking early retirement from the Bengal Nagpur Railway in 1947. He and my mother went to stay with his parents at Rath Drum Farm, Zomba, Malawi. He looked for railway jobs in other countries (one of them was in Nigeria), but was eventually persuaded to stay on the farm and change it from a 'hobby' farm to something commercially viable. In the next 15 years he expanded the dairy herd and started growing flue-cured tobacco.

Always interested in politics, he joined Sir Roy Welensky's Federal Party and was active in the Nyasaland Volunteer Reserve.

He died on 5 March 1963[207], in Zomba, Malawi, at the age of 56. The copy of the certificate .

> *'Death within the Zomba District of the Malawi State; 5ᵗʰ March 1963; Zomba; cerebral haemorrhage; Richard Houston Roan DUNCAN; Rathdrum Farm, Zomba; farmer; British; male; age: 56; length of residence: 14 years; Alan Gilchrist, Medical Supt., Zomba; Reg. 3ʳᵈ April 1963'.*

He was buried on Rath Drum Farm, in the same place as his parents.

---

[207] Malawi Govt. death certificate No.441/2767.

Gravestone of Richard Houston Roan DUNCAN (1906-1963) at Rath Drum Farm, Zomba

MALAWI   GOVERNMENT

The Births and Deaths Registration Act (Cap. 24:01)

	Death within the	ZOMBA			District of the Malaŵi State	
NO. DATE, PLACE AND 41/2767 CAUSE OF DEATH	FULL NAME, ADDRESS, DESCRIPTION AND NATIONALITY OF DECEASED	SEX	AGE	LENGTH OF RESIDENCE IN THE STATE	NAME, ADDRESS AND DESCRIPTION OF INFORMANT	DATE OF REGISTRATION
5TH MARCH, 1963. ZOMBA CEREBRAL HAEMORRHAGE	RICHARD HOUSTON ROAN DUNCAN. RATHDRUM FARM, ZOMBA. FARMER. BRITISH.	M	56	14 YEARS	ALAN GILCHRIST, P.O. BOX 21, ZOMBA. MEDICAL SUPERINTENDENT, ZOMBA.	3RD APRIL, 1963. DISTRICT COMMISSIONER, BY WHOM REGISTERED H.G. DAVIES

GILBERT KONSEKONDE CHIPEMAKINDARegistrar-General at Blantyre, do hereby certify that this is a true copy of the Entry of the Death of RICHARD HOUSTON ROAN
No. _____ 141/2767 _____ according to the return in my custody. Witness my Hand and Seal this _____ 29TH _____ day of _____ OCTOBER 19 85
_____ Registrar-General

R.G. 85370/63M/6.85

Copy of death certificate of Richard Houston Roan DUNCAN (1906-1963)

Richard and Elizabeth DUNCAN had three children:

1. <u>Philippa Hastings Cherry DUNCAN</u> born on 17 August 1932 at Ranchi, India. The baptism record[208] states:

> *'August 17th 1932; village: Ranchi; Jhana: Ranchi; Dist.: Ranchi; Philippa DUNCAN, female; father: Richard Houston Duncan, British, Church of England, Railway Officer; mother: Elisabeth DUNCAN, British, Church of England; giving notice: Richard Houston Duncan, Railway Officer, 11 Godfrey Mansions, Garden Reach, Kidderpore, Calcutta; ...D. Cannell(?), D.T(?).O., B.N. Railway, Kidderpore'.*

<u>*Richard & Elizabeth Duncan, with Philippa and Brian, India (c.1943)*</u>

2. <u>Brian Houston Geoffrey DUNCAN</u> born on 5 March 1934 at Kharagpur, India, and baptised at All Saint's Church, Kharagpur, India[209].

> *'Baptised on 1st April 1934, born 5th March 1934, Brian Houston Geoffry [sic] son of Richard Houston and Elisabeth DUNCAN, abode: 640 Kharagpur, occupation of father: ATO [Asst.Traffic Officer], BNR; A.C.B. Moloney, Chaplain'.*

---

[208] OIOC (N/1/632/5) (reg. 26 July 1946).
[209] OIOC (N/1/556/210).

Duncan family group – Rath Drum Farm 1947 (standing: Richard Duncan & Elizabeth; seated l. to r.: Philippa, Houston, Dulcie, Richard, Brian)

3. <u>Richard Malcolm Hugo DUNCAN</u> born in England on 9 October 1946, educated at Peterhouse, and U. of Rhodesia, and U. of Reading.

Richard DUNCAN divorced Elizabeth (c.1961) and married (2nd, 1962) Anita ROBBINS, known as Ann, daughter of David ROBBINS, and had a daughter:

4. <u>Karen DUNCAN</u> (b.1963) who was born after the death of her father. She is married, has two children, and lives in Malawi.

Ann subsequently married (2nd) Don Pyman, a farmer, and lived near Zomba Malawi.

CHAPTER 8: MARY LEECH AND THE PASLEYS

George Roan DUNCAN I's second marriage was to a widow, **Mary PASLEY (née LEECH)** (c.1821-1855), my 2nd great-grandmother. The descendants of Mary's first marriage to William PASLEY are my relatives too.

The marriage record[210] of George DUNCAN and Mary PASLEY states:

> '*DUNCAN, George Roan; widower; Conductor of Ordnance; 30 December 1840 at Kamptee; PAISLEY* [sic]*, Mary; widow, of Kamptee; Chaplain: Edward Whitehead; Witnesses: H. Theobald, J. Adams.*

The record is then signed by 'G.R. Duncan' and 'M. Pasley'. 'PASLEY' is the correct spelling, because it is used extensively for the children of Mary's 1st marriage (see below). I surmised that Mary's husband would have died not long before her marriage to George Duncan, because young widows were quickly snapped up in India in those days. Searching through the OIOC burial records I found[211]:

> '*Kamptee, 6th May 1840; Sergeant William PASLEY of HM 50th Regiment, was buried by Capt. I.[?] Fitzgerald, HM 50th Regiment*'.

I needed to know whether his widow's name was Mary, so searched through the indexes for a marriage. I eventually found[212]:

> '*Bangalore, 29th April 1835; William PASLEY, Sergeant, HM 39th Regiment, bachelor, and Mary LEECH, spinster, European, were publickly married in the church of Bangalore by banns and with consent of all necessary partners on this Twenty-ninth day of April, eighteen hundred and thirty-five by me, Henry W. Stuart, Junior Chaplain; in the presence of Peece(?) Leech, Maria Smith*' [followed by signatures (transcribed) of William PASLEY and Mary LEECH].

The witness 'Peece LEECH' was probably a parent or sibling of Mary. Who was Maria SMITH – a married sister of Mary, her mother re-married, an aunt?

Note that Mary's husband was known as 'George William' in his daughter Maria's marriage record (see below).

If Mary was born in c.1821 (based on her burial record) she would have been about 14 years old at the time of her first marriage in 1835. In those times in India 14 was not a remarkably young age for marriage.

George William PASLEY and Mary had at least three children, whose baptismal records confirm that they were offspring of the above marriage. I have so far found 10 grandchildren, but there may be more to be 'discovered'. Note that the children were aged 3,2 and 1 when their father died, and they were probably brought up by their mother in the home of their step-father, **George Roan DUNCAN I**.

---

[210] OIOC (N/2/20/235).

[211] OIOC (N/2/20/258).

[212] OIOC (N/2/17/52).

1. <u>Maria (Margaret) PASLEY</u> [GGA] (1836-1862) was born in Bangalore on 22 February 1836. The middle name 'Margaret' appears in the list of Godparents at the baptism of her niece Anna Mary DUNCAN. The baptism record[213] states:

> 'Bangalore; 2nd March 1836; Maria, daughter of William PASLEY, Lance Serjt. H.M. 39th Regiment, and Mary his wife; born on 22nd day of February 1836, was baptized by me (signed) Jas(?) Wright, Senr.Chaplain'.

Maria married, on 26 November 1856 at Sitabuldi, Francis James LAVILLE (c.1834-aft.1860), son of Francis Laville (1799/1801-1869). Francis James was 'a Freemason of high degree'[214]. His father, Francis, was born in Pondicherry in 1801, or in Gascogne, France in 1799. He joined the Madras Garrison Band in 1814, and became Bandmaster Quarter Master Sergeant of the 39th Madras Infantry. He retired in 1851 and became a trader in Singapore, but returned to India and died in Nagpur in 1869. He married (1831) Ellen THOMPSON (1814-1896), the daughter of an Irishman, James Thompson, who became a Conductor of Ordnance, presumably in the Madras Army. Francis and Ellen Laville had eleven children, of whom ten survived to adulthood[215]. One of them was John Ellis LAVILLE, whose great-granddaughter Jessie ETHERINGTON lives in Australia. He had a daughter, Clare Adolphine LAVILLE, whose descendant is married to John BROWN of Norfolk[216]. Another daughter was Josephine Marie LAVILLE, who married (1881) Frederick PHILIPS[217].

Francis James LAVILLE was the eldest surviving child. He became a Superintendent in the Commissioner's Office.

The marriage record[218] states:

> 'Marriages solemnised at Seetabuldee: 26th November 1856; Francis James LAVILLE; age: 22; Bachelor; rank etc.: Clerk in Deputy Commissioner's Office, Nagpore; abode: Seetabuldee; father: Francis Laville; and Maria PASLEY; age: 20; Spinster; abode: Seetabuldee; father: George William Pasley; by licence; witnesses: G. R. Duncan [bride's stepfather], Geo. Collins, Geo. Law, Elizth. Law; Ward Manle, Offg. Minister'.

Maria and Francis had at least two children[219]:

a. <u>Laura Anne LAVILLE</u> [1/2] (1859-aft.1883) was born on 18 September 1859 and baptised at Sitabuldi, Nagpur. The baptisms of her children record her middle name as 'Annie'. The baptism record[220] states:

> 'Baptisms solemnized at Seetabuldee: 9th November 1859; born: 18th Septr. 1859; Laura Anne, daughter of Francis James and Maria LAVILLE, abode: Seetabuldee; clerk; H. Pigot-James, Chaplain'.

---

[213] OIOC (N/2/16/150).

[214] Personal comm. from Susan Laville (Susanlaville@btopenworld.com).

[215] Ibid.

[216] Personal comm.. Reg Laville, 1 April 2004.

[217] OIOC (N/1/177/111).

[218] OIOC (N/2/37/202).

[219] Personal comm. from Sylvia Murphy of Rootsweb India list.

[220] OIOC (N/2/40/279).

Laura married, at All Saints Church, Sitabuldi, Nagpur, on 6 April 1880, John Cochrane COLLINS. The marriage record[221] states:

> *'Marriages solemnized at All Saints Church, Sitabuldi: 1880 April 6th; John Cochrane COLLINS, 23, Bachelor, Accountant, Public Works Department, abode: Nagpore, father: John Collins; and Laura Annie LAVILLE, 20, Spinster, abode: Nagpore; father: Francis James Laville; Banns; witnesses: Mary Ellen Laville [bride's sister?], C. Barclay, Frank J. Laville [bride's father]; F.D. Gray, Chaplain'.*

I could not find a Laura Collins in the 1901 Census. Her death is not in Free BMDs.

Laura is reputed to have had six children. I have found only two, so far:

i) John Laville COLLINS [2/1] (1881-aft.1915/bef.1935) was born on 10 March 1881[222] and baptised at Sitabuldi, Nagpur. The baptism record[223] reads:

> *'Baptisms solemnised at All Saints Church, Sitabuldi; baptised: 1881 April 19th; born: 1881 March 10th; John LAVILLE, son of John Cochrane & Laura Annie Collins; abode: Nagpur; Accountant, Nagpur & Chandigarh State Railway; F.D. Gray, Chaplain, Nagpur'.*

In May 2003 I fortunately made contact with Val Macduff[224], who lives in Perth, WA, and is the granddaughter of Amy Rose WILLIAMS, whose 2nd husband was John Laville Collins. She sent me a photo depicting the couple. Amy had previously been married (1892) to William Thomas Charles INWARD, and had a son (1905-1945).

We know that J. L. Collins worked for the CID, from his marriage record, sent to me by Val.

John married, on 25 April 1915 in Pune (Poona), as her 2nd husband, a widow, Amy Rose INWARD (née WILLIAMS). They had no children[225]. The marriage record states:

> *'Marriages solemnized at St Paul's Church, Poona: 1915 April 28; John Laville COLLINS; 35; Bachelor; Clerk C.I.D. Staff; abode: Poona; father: John Cochrane Collins; and Amy Rose INWARD; 40; widow; abode: Poona; father: John Williams'.*

His death is not in Free BMDs.

---

[221] OIOC (N/1/172/124).
[222] OIOC (N/1/176/41).
[223] OIOC (N/1/176/41).
[224] Val.Macduff@intragis.com.au e-mail (29.5.03).
[225] ibid.

ii) <u>Charlotte Rose COLLINS</u> [2/1] (1883- ?) was born at Sitabuldi on 18 January 1883[226].

> *'Baptisms solemnised at All Saints Church, Sitabuldi; baptised: 1883 February 13th; born: 1883 January 18th; Charlotte Rose, daughter of John Cochran [sic] & Laura Annie[sic] COLLINS; abode: Nagpur; Accountant Public Works Department; F.D. Gray, Chaplain'.*

I could not find Charlotte Rose in the 1901 Census, but she might have married before then in India, or might have died before marriage.

Her marriage and death are not in Free BMDs.

iii) <u>Lewis Cochrane COLLINS</u> [2/1] (1885- ?) was born on 15 January 1885[227].

His marriage and death are not in Free BMDs.

iv) <u>Laura Ellen COLLINS</u> [2/1] (1890- ?) was born on 26 February 1890 and baptised at Quetta (the W. Bengal)[228].

Her marriage and death are not in Free BMDs.

b. <u>'Nelly' (Mary Ellen?) LAVILLE</u> [1/2] (c.1858- ?) who did not marry[229].

Maria and Francis adopted:

c. Jeanette Maria Leish (Leisk?) LAVILLE, daughter of Francis' brother Samuel Laville. She is not related to me (hence her name is not underlined). Jeanette married, on 12 April 1890, at Pune (formerly Poona), James Andrew COLLINS, son of John Collins. James Andrew Collins may have been the brother of John Cochrane Collins, who married Jeanette's adoptive sister Laura Ann Laville, in 1880. James was 'Chief Clerk, Carriage and Wagon Office' presumably in one of the railways. The marriage record[230] states:

> *'Marriages solemnized at St Mary's Church, Poona; 1890 12th April; James Andrew COLLINS; age: full; Bachelor; Chief Clerk Carriage and Wagon Office, Ajmere; abode: Poona; father: John Collins; and Jeanette Maria Leish LAVILLE; age: full; Spinster; father: Samuel Laville; by Banns; witnesses: F.J. Laville [adoptive father], A.C. Owen; P.B. Horne, Chaplain'.*

The witness 'A.C.Owen' may have been one of the Owen family who married Effie Jane Eagles (see Chapter 2).

---

[226] OIOC (N/1/183/42).

[227] IGI.

[228] IGI C750355.

[229] Personal comm.from Susan Laville.

[230] OIOC (N/3/64/283).

There are about twenty Lavilles in the 1881 Census, but none born in India, and none named Francis, which suggests that 'our' Lavilles were a family that had been in India for some time, and may have remained there.

Also, a Maria LAVILLE was born in October-December 1881 at Prestwick (8d, 320)[231].

2. <u>George William PASLEY</u> [GGU] (1837-1898) was born on 12 December 1837 and baptised at Bangalore. The baptism record[232] states:

'Bangalore; 20th December 1837; George, son of William PASLEY, Serjeant, H.M. 39th Regiment, and Mary his wife; born on 12th day of December 1837, was baptized by me (signed) Geo.J. Cubitt, Senr.Chaplain'.

George William PASLEY married (c.1860-1864)[233] probably in Sitabuldi, Maria Elizabeth (MOSS?). I was not sure that this was 'our' George Pasley, because he was baptised 'George'. However, in April 2003 I found the baptism records of his children (see below), which record him as 'George William', and link him to our family through their presence as godparents at the baptism of Mary Moss PASLEY (see below). I have not yet found the marriage record.

George William was a Head Clerk, later Superintendent, in the Inspector General of Police Office, Central Provinces.

George William died on 11 May 1898, in Nagpur, aged 60[234]. His family were recorded as: *'His son, an Inspector of Police in the Central Provinces'*. His property was recorded as *'not known'*.

George William and Maria Elizabeth PASLEY had at least nine children:

a. <u>Mary Margaret PASLEY</u> [1/2] (1861- ?) was born on 9 August 1861 and baptized at Seetabuldee[235]:

'Baptisms solemnized at Seetabuldee: 11th December 1861; born: 9th Augst. 1861; Mary Margaret, Daughter of George William & Maria Elizabeth PASLEY; abode: Seetabuldee; occ.: Clerk, Deputy Commissioner's Office; S.F. Pettigrew, M.A., Chaplain'.

Mary Margaret married Edwin GEORGE, son of Robert George, at Sitabuldi, on 19 September 1883[236]. Edwin was a clerk in the Chief Commissioner's Office in Nagpur.

'Marriages solemnised at All Saints Church, Sitabuldi: 1883 Sept. 19th; Edwin GEORGE, 31(?), Bachelor,Clerk in Chief Commissioner's Office; abode:

[231] Rootsweb's Free BMDs.

[232] OIOC (N/2/16/409).

[233] IGI Film # 1985498.

[234] OIOC (L/AG/34/14a/6/62).

[235] OIOC (N/2/42/308).

[236] OIOC (N/1/185/107).

Nagpur; father: Robert George; Mary Margaret PASLEY, 22, Spinster; abode: Nagpur; father: George Pasley; by Banns; witnesses: Archd. Barclay, G.W. Pasley [father of bride]; Robt. Langford, MA, Chaplain of Kamptee'.

Mary Margaret and Edwin had at least five children:

i) <u>Ethel GEORGE</u> [2/1] (c.1884- ?) was baptised on 24 May 1884 at Sitabuldi[237].

ii) <u>Elsie GEORGE</u> [2/1] (1885- ?) was born on 11 July 1885[238].

iii) <u>Percy Pasley GEORGE</u> [2/1] (1887-1900) was born on 5 June 1887 and baptised at Sitabuldi[239]:

> *'Baptisms solemnized at All Saints Church, Sitabuldi: 1887 Augst. 10th; born: 1887 June 5th; Percy Pasley, son of Edwin & Mary Margaret GEORGE; abode: Nagpur; occ.: Clerk in Chief Commissioner's Office; F.D. Gray, Chaplain'.*

Percy died, aged 13, at Nagpur, of enteric fever[240]:

> *'Burials at Nagpur for the quarter ending 30th September 1900: 1900 August 20; Percy Pasley GEORGE, 13, son of E. George, Clerk Commissioner's Office; buried: 1900 August 20; cause: enteric fever; C.H. Barlow, Chaplain'.*

iv) <u>Gladys GEORGE</u> [2/1] (1889- ?) was born on 21 February 1889[241].

v) <u>Harley Moss GEORGE</u> [2/1] (1891- ?) was born on 29 October 1891, and baptised at Sitabuldi/Nagpur[242]:

> *'Baptisms solemnised at All Saints Church, Sitabuldi & Nagpur: 1891 Decr. 22d; born: 1891 Oct. 29th; Harley Moss, son of Edwin & Mary Margaret GEORGE; abode: Nagpur; occ. Clerk in Chief Commissioner's Office; Arthur E. Stone, Chaplain'.*

b. <u>George William PASLEY II</u> [1/2] (1863-aft.1888) was born on 6 October 1863 and baptized at Sitabuldi[243]:

> *'Baptisms solemnized at Seetabuldee: 25th November 1863; born: 6th Octr. 1863; George William, Son of George William & Maria Elizabeth PASLEY;*

---

[237] IGI.

[238] IGI – C750297.

[239] OIOC (N/1/201/36).

[240] OIOC (N/1/285/155).

[241] IGI.

[242] OIOC (N/1/218/86).

[243] OIOC (N/2/44/273).

abode: Seetabuldee; occ.: Head Clerk in Office of Inspector General of Police, Central Province; Alexander Taylor, M.A., Chaplain'.

It seems that 'George William' became 'William George', rather as my grandfather was baptised 'George Houston' but became 'Houston George'. In both cases this was probably to prevent confusion between son and father.

William worked for the police in the Central Provinces, as indicated in his father's death notice (see above), and his marriage record. However, in the baptism record of his daughter, he is described as working for the railway police.

William George Pasley married, on 11 May 1885 at Jabalpur, Amelia LIMA (c.1866-aft.1888), daughter of Edwin Lima[244]:

> *'Marriages solemnized at Christ Church, Jubbulpore, Central Provinces; 1885 May 11; William George PASLEY, 22, Bachelor; Headquarters, Inspector of Police, Jubbulpore; father: George Pasley; and Amelia LIMA, 19, Spinster; abode: Jubbulpore; father: Edwin Lima, by Licence; witnesses: E. Lima [father?], J.H. Bloomfield, M. Ram; M. Lambert, Chaplain'.*

They had at least one child:

> i) <u>Maud Violet PASLEY</u> [2/1] (1888- ?) was born on 1 October 1888 and baptised at Jabalpur[245]:
>
> > *'Baptisms solemnized at Christ Church, Jabalpur, C.P.: 1888 Novr. 14th; born: 1888 October 1st; Maud Violet, Daughter of William George & Amelia PASLEY; abode: Khundwah; occ.: Inspector Railway Police; W. Henry Bray, Chaplain'.*

c. <u>Ada Maria PASLEY</u> [1/2] (1865- ?) was born on 27 September 1865, and baptised at Sitabuldi[246]:

> *'Baptisms solemnized at Seetabuldee: 1865 Novr. 9th; 1865 Septr. 27th; Ada Maria, Dau. of George William & Maria Elizabeth PASLEY; abode: Seetabuldee; occ.of father: Superintendent of Inspector's General of Police Office, Central Provinces; Alexander Taylor, M.A., Chaplain'.*

d. <u>Henry Moss PASLEY</u> [1/2] (1867- ?) was born on 12 June 1867 and baptised at Sitabuldi[247]:

> *'Baptisms solemnized at Nagpur, Seetabuldee: 1867 July 13th; 1867 April 24th; Henry Moss, Son of George William & Maria Margaret [sic] PASLEY, abode:*

---

[244] OIOC (N/1/192/81).

[245] OIOC (N/1/206/34).

[246] OIOC (N/1/114/326).

[247] OIOC (N/1/121/53).

Seetabuldee; occ.of father: Superintendent of Inspector General of Police Office, Central Provinces; Thos. A.E. Pratt, Chaplain'.

e. <u>Minnie Laura PASLEY</u> [1/2] (1871- ?) was born on 17 March 1871 and baptised on 17 April 1871 at Sitabuldi[248]. She was 'discovered' by me in April 2004.

f. <u>Henry Duncan PASLEY</u> [1/2] (bef.1873-aft.1894) was of 'full age', i.e. 21, when he married in 1894. I have not yet found his baptism record, but place him in this gap between siblings.

He married, on 25 May 1894 in the Central Provinces of India, Emily Lucy Helen BEATSON, daughter of William Walter Beatson[249]:

> *'Church of England returns, Central Provinces: 1894 May 25th; Henry Duncan PASLEY; age: Full; Bachelor; occ.: Railway Inspector of Police; abode: Dondargarh; father: George William Pasley; and Emily Lucy Helen BEATSON; age: full; Spinster; abode: Saugor; father: William Walter Beatson; by Banns; witnesses: L.E. Karlson, A.E. Mortimer, H.R. Beatson; V.W. Kinsman, Chaplain'.*

It is possible that the witnesses '*L.E.Karlson*' and '*A.E.Mortimer*' were married sisters of the groom.

g. <u>May Moss PASLEY</u> [1/2] (1873- ?) was born on 24 March 1873 and baptised at All Saints Church, Sitabuldi[250]:

> *'Baptisms solemnized at All Saints Church, Seetabuldee: 1873 April 25th; born: 1873 March 24th; Mary Moss, Daughter of George William & Maria Elizabeth PASLEY; abode: Seetabuldee; occ.of father: Superintendent of Inspector General of Police Office, Central Provinces; G.F. Carruthers, M.A., Chaplain of Seetabuldee; Godparents: Thomasina Duncan, Mary Faith Duncan, George Roan Duncan'.*

The godmother '*Thomasina Duncan*' was the niece of Mary Pasley's 2nd husband, **George Roan DUNCAN I** (see Chapter 2). She had been married to her cousin, William George DUNCAN [GGU] (1844-1872), and had been widowed in February 1872. '*Mary Faith Duncan*' was the half sister of George William Pasley, the child's father. '*George Roan Duncan*' might have been the child's grandfather, **George Roan DUNCAN I**, or **George Roan DUNCAN II**, the child's half uncle. Note that her cousin William Duncan GORDON (b.1871) was baptised at the same ceremony.

---

[248] IGI Batch C750224.

[249] OIOC (N/1/237/179).

[250] OIOC (N/1/144/56).

h. Margaret Jane PASLEY [1/2] (1875- ?) was born on 6 October 1875 and baptised at All Saints Church, Sitabuldi[251]:

> 'Baptisms solemnized at All Saints Church, Sitabuldi: 1875 Novr. 19th; born: 1875 October 6th; Margaret Jane, Daughter of George William & Maria Elizabeth PASLEY; abode: Nagpur; Superintendent of Inspector General of Police Office, Central Provinces; M.E. Mills, Chaplain'.

i. Alice Mildred PASLEY [1/2] (1880- ?) was born on 18 December 1880 and baptised on 18 December 1880 in All Saints Church, Sitabuldi[252]:

> 'Baptisms solemnised at All Saints Church, Sitabuldi, 1880 December 18th, born: 1880 October 28th; Alice Mildred, Daughter of George William & Maria Elizabeth PASLEY; abode: Nagpur; occ.: Pensioner, Late Superintendent, Office of the Inspector Genl.of Police; T.D. Gray, Chaplain'.

There was also a James Duncan PASLEY, married in 1862[253] to a Jane HALL. He was the son of James PASLEY, according to the marriage record. The father might have been a brother of George William PASLEY.

James Duncan and Jane PASLEY had:

a. Duncan Quinton Williamson PASLEY (1867- ?) born on 10 August 1867 at Prince of Wales Island (Penang)[254].

3. Eliza PASLEY [GGA] (1839- ?) was born in Bellary on 6 July 1839, less than a year before her father died. The baptism record[255] states:

> 'Bellary; 7th August 1839; Eliza, daughter of William PASLEY, Serjt. H.M. 39th Regiment, and Mary his wife; born on 6th July 1839, was baptized by me (signed) E.R. Ottey, Senr.Chaplain'.

I could not find Eliza in the 1901 Census.

It is quite possible that Eliza died in infancy, because Mary Pasley's first child by her second husband (George Roan DUNCAN I) was named Eliza.

Note that the 1881 Census has, at Burnfoot, Preston Road, Preston, Lancs.:

> PASLEY, George B.   49 (b.c.1832)   b. East Indies   Bengal Civil Service, ret'd.

---

[251] OIOC (N/1/154/57).

[252] OIOC (N/1/174/49).

[253] OIOC (N/1/102/79).

[254] OIOC (N/1/121/44).

[255] OIOC (N/2/19/132).

PASLEY, Ellen A.   47 (b.c.1834)   b. East Indies   wife

PASLEY, Edward H. = QUIN, Caroline (1895) N/1/261/5
PASLEY, M.W.S.   = St JOHN, Grace (1891) N/1/221/24

There are numerous PASLEYs in the 1881 Census, but only two others born in India, living at 'Woodbourne', Eastbourne, namely: Kate H. PASLEY (b.c.1842) and her daughters: Mary L. PASLEY (b.c. 1861) born in India, and Florence PASLEY (b.c.1872) born in Montrose, Scotland. Kate must have been quite well off, because she had a governess and three servants.

A Dr Gilbert PASLEY was Physician General in Madras.

APPENDIX A. TRANSCRIPT OF TWO LETTERS FROM ROBERT DUNCAN.

The following are transcripts of two letters from Robert DUNCAN to his brother, George Roan DUNCAN I. I have amended the punctuation, but have not altered the paragraphing and capital letters.

LETTER NO. 1 (RD1):

Limerick

July 6th 1866 (1867)[2]

My Dear George[1],

I have just received your kind letter of the 7th May last, from the widow of our late Dear Brother Thomas[3]. The poor fellow died at Clonmel three years ago. He left his Daughter and Wife well provided for.

Our brother John[4] is also dead. He went to America several years ago and died there.

Captain Kennedy[5] died a short time since and left Lydia[6] very comfortable. Rebecca[7] is also in very good circumstances and has been receiving the rent of the Roscrea[8] property (which is yours) since our mother's death in 1833. The three of us with yourself are the only members of our family now alive.

I regret exceedingly to have to let you know that I am the only one of them that is not well off. I have been treated very badly by Richard Ely[9], who was the means of depriving me of my farm and house at Ballaghmore[10], he being anxious to secure the whole place to himself. But God did not let him enjoy it long.

I was obliged to take a situation at Major M. Fitt & Sons Brewery, Limerick, with whom I have been living during the last 14 years on a very small salary, only a few shillings a week, barely sufficient to support my large family and myself.

I assure you that I have suffered very much, and the very life was nearly worked out of me. And what is worse, my best friend "Old Mr Fitt" died a few weeks ago, and I have been discharged. As one of the Young New has taken my place in the Brewery I think that I was thought to be getting too old. I was treated unkindly after my long service, but if old Mr Fitt had lived I would not have been discharged. I am now totally without any means, and I do not know what to do, as I find it impossible to get a situation, and my poor wife and daughter are nearly heart broken as we fear that we will be soon without a home, the Landlord having threatened (?) to seize for the rent which is due. If I had as much as would enable me to get into business in a small way we could struggle on very well during the few years we have to live in this world.

My daughter[11] is a most industrious Girl, and a better child is not in existence. My son George[12] is serving in the police in Leeds. He is a fine looking man, over 6 feet in height. My nephew Thomas Woodlock[13], who is an officer like yourself, and now Lieut. And 2nd Master of the Waterford Artillery Militia, Waterford, got George his present appointment, and he would do everything in his power for me, but his pay is very small at present. He was happy to hear that you were a Captain in the Army[14]. I often mentioned your name to him in hopes that he might try to find out whether you were alive and where you were serving, but he could not find out your address.

I hope, My Dear George, that you will not fail in doing something for me soon. A few pounds would be of the greatest service at present to pay my rent.

I am joined by all friends in love to you and all your family, and hope to have the pleasure of hearing from you an a short time, when I will in return let you know all the particulars not mentioned in this letter.

I remain, My Dear George, Your Ever Affectionate Brother

Robert Duncan

PS Direct your Letter to the care of Major (Messrs?) Fitt & Sons, Newgate Brewery, Limerick

LETTER NO.2 (RD2):

No. 3 Westland Street,
Limerick
13th March 1867

My Dearest George,

It has given me great pleasure to receive your kind and affectionate letter dated 29th January last, which arrived here on the 10th instant, and I assure you, my Dear Brother, that we are all delighted beyond measure to hear that Mrs Duncan[15] intends to come to this country very soon. Nothing will give us so much happiness as to have her with us for some time, and believe me that we will do our utmost to make her as comfortable as possible, but my only fear is that any house will not be half good enough for her. Thomasina would be glad to go meet her Dear Aunt after her arrival from India if you should wish her to do so.

I am glad to hear that your son William[16] is such a fine young man as you represent, and I am sure that Thomasina would be as happy to see him as he'd be to see her. You are quite right in saying that I would have no objection to their corresponding. On the contrary, I am happy at their doing so, and trust that it may lead to a happy result if such is God's will. I think that William will find Thomasina everything he could desire. I must say that a better natured or more affectionate Girl is not to be found. We should be delighted if William would come to Limerick with his dear mother.

I am sure, my Dear Brother, that you will be sorry to hear that I am still out of employment. I have made application for several situations but the answer I received was "You are too old". I do not know on earth what to do or how to manage; only for your kind assistance we would have been in a very bad way during last winter. I and my poor wife feel very much for being situated as we are, and only for the late Richard Ely we would be now in prosperous circumstances, as he was the sole cause of our being deprived of our farm at Ballaghmore, to secure it for himself, which God did not let him enjoy long. But I forgive him all the serious injury he did me.

If I had now a few pounds to enable me to get a small farm, or to get into business in a small way, I and my poor wife would be happy and contented during the remainder of our life.

I very seldom see …… sisters. They are too pr….. visit me as I suppose they …..are too poor. They have not given me the least assistance, although they are very comfortable at Kilkee[17], a beautiful sea bathing place. You ask me how old you are. I think that you are about 66, as you were nearly 17 when you joined the Army[18]. Thank God you have got on so well and enjoy such good health.

I now conclude, and am joined by Anne and Thomasina in ….love to you and all your family.

Your affectionate and loving Brother

Robert Duncan

I hope to have the pleasure of hearing from you soon.

Notes:

(1)   George Roan DUNCAN (c. 1799-c.1898), gg grandfather of Philippa, Brian and Richard.

(2)   The date is not clear.

(3)   I have no information about Thomas DUNCAN.

(4)   I have no information about John DUNCAN. I have found two John DUNCANs in Irish records:

John DUNCAN m. Miss Jane AGNEW, Londonderry (September 1808), and John DUNCAN of Armagh m. Miss Isabella WRIGHT, Dublin (17 August 1818). The latter is more probable.

(5)   Lydia DUNCAN m. Capt. Francis KENNEDY on 18 May 1835, in St. Michael's, Limerick, Ireland.

(6)   Lydia DUNCAN is presumably the sister of Robert, and of George Roan DUNCAN. There was a Lydia DUNCAN who witnessed the wedding of Mary Faith DUNCAN to Mr DE LA HOYDE, in India, on 20 July 1875. This might have been this Lydia, i.e. a witness at her niece's wedding. However, I think it is more likely that George Roan DUNCAN (this Lydia's brother) had a daughter named Lydia, and that it was she who witnessed her sister's wedding.

(7)   Rebecca DUNCAN is presumably the sister of Robert, and of George Roan DUNCAN, and is probably named after her mother, Rebecca DUNCAN (née ROANE). A Rebecca DUNCAN married William JOHNSON (or JOHNSTON) in Drumcree, Co. Armagh in 1828, but I have no proof this is the same person.

(8)   Roscrea is a town in Co. Tipperary, about 35 miles (50-60 km) ENE of Limerick, and 40 miles SW of Dublin.

(9)   A George ELY married a Lydia ROANE in 1780. It's possible that this Lydia ROANE was a sister of Rebecca ROANE, and thus the aunt of Robert DUNCAN. Thus George ELY would have been Robert's uncle (by marriage). The Richard ELY mentioned in the letter might have been George's brother.

(10)   Ballaghmore is a common place name in Ireland. Candidates are:

County	Civil Parish	Poor Law Union
Antrim	Ballymoney	Ballymoney
Antrim	Dunluce	Coleraine
Carlow	Myshall	Carlow
Fermanagh	Rossorry	Enniskillin
Laois	Stradbally	Athy
Laois	Kyle	Roscrea

I think the last in the list is the most likely, but have not been able to locate it on a map.

(11)   I suggest this is Thomasina DUNCAN, mentioned by name in the second letter.

(12)   The 1881 Census records, at 12 Briar St., Linthorpe, Yorks.:

George DUNCAN, head, 51, b. Ireland; charging .... (iron)
Nellie DUNCAN, wife, 48, b. Ireland
John DUNCAN, son, 21, b. Ireland, engine driver
Robert DUNCAN, son, 16, b. Leeds, errand boy
Florence DUNCAN, dau., 14, b. Leeds

George W. DUNCAN, son, 11, b. Middlesborough

The above suggests that this might be the George DUNCAN referred to in the letter, since two children were born in Leeds. If so, George DUNCAN left Ireland after 1860 (when his son John was born) and before 1865 (when his son Robert was born). If this is the "right" George DUNCAN, one would have to presume that he left the police force.

(13)   Thomas WOODLOCK may have been the son of Rebecca (Robert's sister), or the son of Robert's wife's brother. In the latter case, Robert's wife would have been born Anne WOODLOCK. Because Thomas WOODLOCK was an officer, it should be possible to trace his parents from the military records in the PRO.

(14)   George Roan DUNCAN I was commissioned as a Lieutenant in 1856, i.e. when 57 years old. He was still listed as a Lieutenant in 1888, so Captain may have been a temporary rank.

(15)   George Roan DUNCAN I married three times.

(16)   From 'Baptisms solemnised at the Chaplain's Station within the Archdeaconry of Madras': William George DUNCAN; baptised on 15 September 1844; said to be born: 27 August 1844; son of George Roan and Mary DUNCAN; parents' abode: Nagpore; father's profession: Conductor on Depot.

(17)   Kilkee is on the west coast of Ireland, in Co. Clare, more or less W of Limerick.

(18)   According to records in the OIOC, George Roan DUNCAN was born in the Parish of Birr (Parsonstown), King's County, Ireland. He arrived in Madras on 30 January 1817 on 'Herefordshire', aged 18. He lived to 90, married three times, and fathered at least 11 children. Birr is a town in the present Co. Offaly, on the border with Co. Tipperary.

APPENDIX B: TESTIMONIALS OF GEORGE ROAN DUNCAN

TITLES OF THE MADRAS EUROPEAN REGIMENT

1742	Madras Europeans.
1766	1st Madras Europeans
1774	1st Madras European Regiment
1779	The Madras European Regiment
1799	2nd Madras European Regiment disbanded.
1824	The Regiment was divided/re-formed into 1st and 2nd (presumably battalions).
1839	1st Madras (European) Regiment absorbed the 2nd Battalion.
1842	2nd Madras (European) Light Infantry.
1843	1st Madras (European) Fusiliers
1859	1st Madras Fusiliers (under Crown control, after the Indian Mutiny)
1862	102nd Regiment of Foot (Royal Madras Fusiliers), transferred to the British Army.
1881	united with 103rd Reg't.of Foot to become 1st Batt. The Royal Dublin Fusiliers.

TESTIMONIALS

OBTAINED BY LIEUT. GEORGE ROAN DUNCAN, DEPUTY ASSISTANT COMMISSARY OF ORDNANCE, DURING THE PERIOD PASSED IN THE SERVICE OF THE GOVERNMENT, FROM THE YEAR 1816.

EXTRACT from Regimental Orders by Major J.F. GIBSON (late Major General), Commanding 2nd Madras European Regiment – Dated Camp Kamptee, 2nd March 1829:

"It is but due to Serjeant-Major George Duncan also to record the high sense which Major Gibson entertains of the irreproachable character and conduct of this intelligent Non-Commissioned Officer, and Major Gibson can assure him that it will afford him pleasure, should it ever be in his power, to further the Serjeant-Major's prospects in the service". "A true Extract"

(Signed) J.G. Neill, Lieut.and Adjutant, Madras European Regiment.

"I do hereby certify that I have known Sub-Conductor George Duncan of the Ordnance Department (formerly in the Madras European Regiment) since the year 1825, and I have always considered him a man of most excellent character. From April 1826 to April 1831 when I was Adjutant to the Regiment, he was under my immediate orders, for the first few months as clerk in the Adjutant's department, and the rest of the time as Serjeant-Major to the Regiment, during the whole of which time he evinced a zeal and attention to his duties highly creditable to himself and beneficial to the discipline of the Regiment".

(Signed) E. Simpson, Lieut., Madras European Regiment, Kamptee, 11th August 1835.

"This is to certify that I have known Sub-Conductor George Duncan for nearly nine years, five of which he was with the late 2nd European Regiment, and was Serjeant Major during the greater part of that time, and I know that he gave great satisfaction in that arduous and important situation, and at the same time gained the good wishes and respect of both officers and men of the Regiment. I have always considered him a most respectable and deserving character".

(Signed) J.C. Hawes, Lieut. and Quarter Master, Madras European Regiment, Kamptee, 11th August 1835.

"At the request of Mr Conductor Duncan I have much pleasure in certifying, that during the time he has served in the Ordnance Department under me for the long period of twelve years, he has conducted himself in a very exemplary manner, and is a very intelligent and experienced Warrant Officer".

(Signed) A. Hyslop, Major, Commissary of Ordnance, Nagpore Subsidiary Force, Nagpore, 8th February 1844.

EXTRACT from Departmental Orders by Major W.H. Miller, Commissary of Ordnance:

"To Permanent Conductor Duncan, the Major's acknowledgments are in an especial manner, due, for the very zealous and efficient manner in which the duties of the various important charges he has held in the Department have been conducted by him. His intelligence, ability, and indefatigable assiduity in his present confidential and highly responsible situation, have been most marked, and rendered him a very valuable Assistant to the Commissary in the performance of his own duties, for which he requests Mr Duncan to accept his best thanks".

(Signed) H.H. Miller, Captain, Commissary of Ordnance, Nagpore Subsidiary Force, Seetabuldee, 14th July 1851.

"I have known Mr G. Duncan, Deputy Assistant Commissary of Ordnance to the Nagpore Irregular Force for a period of thirteen years, and have always held him in much respect. For nine years I was associated with him as a member of the Poor Fund Committee and had ample opportunities of forming a personal opinion of the Character. I have heard Officers of all ranks, his official superiors and others speak of him in terms of praise. He was held in esteem by the successive Residents of Nagpur under whom I served at the Court, and I have great pleasure, at his request, in affording this testimony to the merits of so deserving an individual".

(Signed) G. Ramsay, Residency Resident of the Court of Nepaul, Nov. 15th 1855

"At the request of Mr. Conductor Duncan, now Acting Assistant Commissary of Ordnance Nagpur Irregular Force, I have much pleasure in stating that I have known him for upwards of twenty years, three years and half of which he was under my immediate Command as Permanent Conductor in the Arsenal at Seetabuldee. During that time he conducted himself in the most exemplary manner shewing himself to be a most intelligent and zealous Warrant Officer, most trustworthy, and he has to my knowledge always enjoyed the complete confidence of his superiors. He has been recommended for

some years past by my Predecessor, Major Miller, and myself in the Annual Recommendations Rolls of the Department, as most deserving of Promotion to the Commissioned Rank, to which it would give me the greatest satisfaction to see him raised".

(Signed) H.H. Bell, Seetabuldee, 6th December 1855; Commissary of Ordnance, Nagpur Forces.

Copy of a letter from Col. N.H. Miller,, Madras Artillery, dated Ootacamund 26th August 1857:

"Sir:- In reply to your letter asking me for a testimonial to your Character with a view to such assisting you in obtaining a Commission, I have to say that I know of few things that would give me greater pleasure than seeing you Gazetted for one, and I shall be truly happy if I can be in any way instrumental towards your attaining the object of your wishes. Our acquaintance commenced above thirty two years ago (in 1825) when you were Serjeant Major of the then 2nd Madras European Regiment under Major (the late Major General Gibson) who I know entertained the highest possible opinion of you. In consequence of my personal intimacy with that officer, and with three Adjutants of the Regiment, Lieutenants French, Paget and Simpson, I had constant opportunities of seeing you at their quarters, and of learning what they thought of you, and I well remember having often heard you spoken of, by one and all of them, as one of the best Serjeant-Majors in the Service. It was with no slight satisfaction, therefore, that on my joining the Arsenal at Nagpur in June 1844, I found, you attached to it as a Conductor, and I am bound to say that my anticipation, founded on my previous knowledge of you, in regard to finding you a most able, intelligent and trustworthy assistant in the performance of my duties, were fully realized during the seven years you were under my command. Throughout that long period, your unwearied attention to your duties (generally arduous enough) your zeal, ability, integrity and thoroughly soldier-like demeanour on all occasions, elicited my most cordial approbation. If I mistake not, I have more than once placed this on official record, to which I think you might with propriety refer, when making your application for the Commission, which, I very earnestly and sincerely hope will be conferred on you".

(Signed) W.H. Miller Colonel, Madras Artillery.

"I have known Mr. Duncan for more than 35 years as I was in the Madras European Regiment in which he rose to be Sergeant-Major when I was also in the Regiment. His unvaried sobriety, good conduct and high respectability, gained the good opinion of his superiors, and when I left the Regiment I was acquainted with Mr. Duncan for some years when he was in the Ordnance Department at Seetabuldee, during which period I know that he was very much respected. Mr. Duncan having been selected to officiate as Deputy Assistant Commissary of Ordnance to the Nagpur Irregular Force, is a proof of his having sustained the character I knew him to possess for many years previous, and I consider him a very faithful servant of Government".

(Signed) William Hill, Brigadier, Comg. Hy. Contingent, Bolarum, 18th May 1857.

"I have known Mr. Duncan for upwards of thirty years, and willingly bear testimony to the high character he has always borne. He was Serjeant-Major of the 2nd European Regiment after the division of the old Madras European Regiment in 1824, and gave great satisfaction from the zeal and ability with which he performed his duties. I consider Mr. Duncan as a most deserving man and shall

be glad if this testimonial can be of any benefit in assisting to obtain for him that reward which his character and length of service lead him to expect".

(Signed) Thos. A. Duke, Colonel, Comg. The Troops in Garrison, Madras, 28th August 1857.

Extract from a letter No. 904 dated 19th October 1857, from Major Arrow, Commanding Nagpur Irregular Force, to G.A.C. Plowden Esqr., Commissioner of Nagpur.

"I gladly avail myself of the opportunity to bear testimony to the merits of that highly respectable and most deserving Warrant Officer.

The numerous testimonials to his zeal, integrity and ability in the discharge of his public duties, appended to Mr. Duncan's Memorial, renders any lengthened encomium on my part quite unnecessary, but I may be permitted to say that Mr. Duncan has fully maintained the high character given him by his many superiors during the period he has been under my Command, and that I consider him to be a most trustworthy and efficient Government Servant".

'A True Extract'. Signed: J.C. Day, Brigade Major, Nagpur Irregular Force.

"I have much pleasure to declare in certifying that for nearly five years I have had opportunities of associating with Lieutenant George Duncan of the Madras Veteran Establishment, and Deputy Assistant Commissary of Ordnance of the Nagpur Irregular Force, who is about to solicit promotion to the rank of Captain; and both from my own observation and from what I have heard from others concerning this highly respectable, deserving old officer, who is still unusually hale after his long service of 44 years, I should greatly rejoice to be in any way instrumental in obtaining the above rank for him".

Signed A. Henry E. Boileau, Colonel, Commandant of the Bengal Engineers, Nagpur, 22nd August 1860

"It gives me truest pleasure to declare in writing the very high opinion I entertain and have entertained of you since our acquaintance began six years ago, and of however little value it may be, you are most welcome to all I can say and to all I can do (if that be anything) to further your very natural and very laudable ambition. I only hope Her Majesty's Government may be as fully convinced, as I am, of your merits as a soldier, your worth as a man, and your principles as a gentleman. You served in conjunction with me at Sonegaon, and afterwards under my immediate command, as attached to the Battery in this Force, and I can truly say that no other officer could have been appointed in whom I had greater confidence or who I felt assured would do what there was to be done with greater zeal than yourself. As you are still in possession of good health and a sound constitution, I trust you may yet long be spared to enjoy whatever honors may be awarded you, and though many may be more powerful to advance your interest, none will be more delighted to hear of your advancement".

(Signed) E.M. Playfair, Captain, Commandant of Artillery, Nagpur Irregular Force, Taklee, 31st August 1860.

"I have known you for the last 14 years, and am well aware of the esteem you are held in by all who are acquainted with you. By a long and faithful service you have fairly earned what you seek for and had I any interest with the Heads of Departments through which your Memorial must pass, I should gladly exert it in your support, as it is I can only give you the best wishes of an old soldier for the success of another".

(Signed) R.T. Snow, Brevet-Major, 24th Regiment Madras Native Infantry, & Deputy Commissioner, Nagpur.

Seetabuldee, 24th September 1860.

"I am of opinion that you are about to take a very proper step in submitting a memorial to Her Majesty's Government, soliciting promotion to the rank of Captain, a boon which hope your long and approved good service, extending over a period of 44 years, is certain to secure for you. The numerous and very handsome testimonials which you possess from officers of every rank who had known you long and well in the different grades which you have filled in the service, all alike testifying to your exemplary character and conduct, and to the zeal and attention with which you have discharged the duties (many of them of a highly important nature) that devolved upon you, must be of much more value and weight than any thing I can say, but at the same time I willingly add my good word to theirs, and I shall be extremely glad if it should in any way tend towards assisting you in the attainment of your wishes.

I had the pleasure of first making your acquaintance six years ago, when I joined the Nagpore Commission, at which time you held the responsible post of Permanent Conductor in the Arsenal at Seetabuldee, and from all I saw of you in personal communications, as well as from what I heard of your character and qualifications from numerous friends, and especially from the officer who was then Commissary of Ordnance of Nagpore Force. I was truly glad when you obtained the appointment which you now hold, and none of your numerous well wishers were more pleased than I was to congratulate you on subsequently receiving your Commission as Lieutenant on the Veteran Establishment, to which I need only add that I esteem you so highly as an old fellow-soldier and brother officer, that it will afford me sincere pleasure to see you, as I trust soon to do, advanced to the rank of Captain".

(Signed) J.K. Spence, Major, Deputy Commissioner & Superintendent of Police, Nagpore Province, 25th September 1860.

"I have the greatest pleasure in thus bearing my testimony to the wonderful energy and marked coolness displayed by Lieutenant Duncan on the night of the 13th June 1857.

This gallant old officer on hearing of the outbreak at Nagpore, at once proceeded to the Arsenal, and there made every preparation to meet the expected attack of the insurgents. During the night he also patrolled the various roads leading to the city, and single handed gallantly attacked and disarmed a rebel Sowar.

His conduct on this, as I believe it has on all other occasions, drew forth the highest praise from those who knew how bravely he had done his duty on that eventful night"

(Signed) William J. Morris, Captain, 2nd in Command Nagpore Irregular Cavalry, 27th September 1860.

"I know not how I can aid you, beyond expressing my hearty good wishes for your success, in obtaining the honorable distinction you so justly covet, as the reward of your long and faithful service in every grade.

I have known you since 1853, I have already heard you spoken of in terms of the greatest respect and regard by the different officers of the Nagpore Force, and I can bear personal testimony to the truth of Captain Morris's statement as to your gallant conduct on the memorable night of the 13th June 1857".

(Signed) W.W. Heude, Civil Surgeon, Nagpur, 28th September 1860.

"It gives me great pleasure to be able to say a few words in your favour in case they may be of any use to you, and I shall be very glad to hear that you have obtained your Captaincy, a distinction, which considering your long and faithful service in my opinion you well deserve.

I can testify to the careful manner in which you conducted all the arrangements connected with the taking over charge of the Arsenal and Magazine Stores of the late Rajah of Nagpore in 1854. Your conduct at that time I have reason to know, as I was then Brigade Major to the Irregular Force, gave every satisfaction. I can further state that your promptitude and tact in carrying out Mr. Plowden's orders for destroying a lot of powder and ammunition at Sonegaon, shortly after the intended mutiny at Nagpore, was much approved of by Mr. Plowden. Wishing you every success".

(Signed) A.B. Cumberlege, Captain, Assistant to Governor-General's Agent, Nagpore, 30th September 1860.

Copy of letter No. 32 of 1860, from Major E.K. Elliot, Commissioner, Nagpore; to Colonel H. Marshall, Military Secretary to Government, Fort Saint George. Dated: Nagpore 19th October 1860.

"Sir.- In transmitting for the purpose of being laid before the Government of Fort Saint George a copy of letter from the Officer Commanding Nagpore Irregular Force, No. 830 under date the 17th instant, submitting in triplicate a memorial and testimonials from Lieutenant George Duncan of the Veteran Establishment and Deputy Assistant Commissary of Ordnance, Nagpure Force, I have the honor most earnestly to recommend the prayer of the memorialist to the favorable consideration of His Honor the Governor in Council.

Lieutenant Duncan has served the state well and faithfully during a period of 44 years. He had earned the respect and good will of all with whom he has been associated, as will be seen from a perusal of the annexures attached to his memorial.

In 1854 when Officiating as Commissioner of the Province, I submitted his name for the appointment in the Nagpur Irregular Force which he now holds, and for which I selected him from my personal knowledge of his conduct and character.

In the year 1858, he was promoted to the Rank of a Lieutenant on the Veteran Establishment, and he now seeks for advancement to the grade of Captain, a boon which I trust will be accorded to him in acknowledgement of his merits as a faithful soldier and a good man".

I have the honor to be Sir, Your Most Obedient Servant (Signed) E.K. Elliot,- Commissioner of Nagpore.

Copy of letter No.35, From Major E.K. Elliott, Commissioner of Nagpore; to Colonel H. Marshall, Military Secretary to Government, Fort St. George, dated: Nagpore, 11th December 1860.

"Sir.- With reference to your office letter No.2712, dated 2nd October 1855, I have now the honor to report for the information of the Honorable the Governor in Council, the completion of the duties for which the services of Lieutenant Duncan, Officiating Deputy Commissary of Ordnance, were placed at the disposal of the Commissioner in 1854-55, he is therefore available for re-employment under the Madras Government.

In justice to Lieutenant Duncan, I would wish to place on record the zeal and efficiency with which he has performed his duties during the period he has been attached to the Nagpore Irregular Force.

Lieutenant Duncan has served at this station for upwards of 38 years, and having expressed a wish to be posted to the Arsenal at Seetabuldee, I would esteem it a favor if His Excellency the Commander-in-Chief could as a mark of approbation, so arrange as to meet the wishes of this old soldier". (Signed) E.K. Elliot, Commissioner.

Extract from the Force Orders No.1, dated 5th February 1861.

"The services of Lieutenant Duncan, Deputy Assistant Commissary of Ordnance of this Force, having been placed agreeably to instructions from the Commissioner at the disposal of the Madras Government, the Officer Commanding the Force has much pleasure in putting on record the valuable services of that Officer from the first formation of this force, viz. October 1854 until this date".

'A True Extract' (Signed) Thos. Wakefield, Captain, Brigade Majore, Nagpore Irregular Force.

[The above are] 'True Copies and Extracts' L.F.C. Thomas, Major, Commissary of Ordnance, Nagpore Force.

APPENDIX C: DESCENDANTS OF ELLEN CAMPION (nee DUNCAN)

I 'found' Ellen Campion II in 2003 through her marriage record. These children were very young when Ellen died in 1851, ranging from 11 years to only three weeks. I presume they were brought up by Jeremiah's 3rd wife.

a. <u>Ellen CAMPION II</u> [1/2] (c.1840-1861/67) was born in about 1840, based on her age at marriage (see below).

Ellen married at Jalna [Jaulnah], India, on 29 December 1859, William George PEACOCK (c.1832-aft.1861), son of Thomas Peacock[256]:

> *'Marriages solemnised at Jaulnah: 29th December 1859; William George PEACOCK, 27, Bachelor, Clerk, Resident's Political Office, Jaulnah; father: Thomas Peacock; Ellen CAMPION, 19, Spinster, abode: Jaulnah; father: Jeremiah Campion; by Banns; witnesses: J. Campion [father?], V.E.R. Ardagh, S.R. Campion; Ed. Kilvert, AB, Chaplain'.*

The witness 'V.E.R. Ardagh' was Vernon Edmund Russell ARDAGH, who I noticed in a record on the same microfilm. He was a Sub-Asst. Surgeon at the time. The witness 'S.R. Campion' must be the bride's sister, Sarah Rebecca CAMPION (b.1845).

William George Peacock was a clerk in the Resident's Political Office (1859, 1st marriage record – above), later, Assistant Secretary to a Minister to His Highness the Nizam (of Hyderabad?)(1868, 2nd marriage record), and later, Assistant Private Secretary to HE the Prime Minister (of Hyderabad?)(1871, baptism of son).

Ellen and William had at least one child:

i) <u>William Henry Campion PEACOCK</u> [2/1] (1861- ?) was born on 8 May 1861 and baptised in Bolarum (near Secunderabad)[257]:

> *'Baptisms solemnised at Bolarum: 21 September 1861; born: 8 May 1861; William Henry Campion, son of William and Ellen PEACOCK; abode: Chudderghaut; occ.: Clerk in the Resident's Office; H. Pigot James, Chaplain'.*

<u>Family names to give priority to</u>:

William, Henry, George, Thomas, Campion, Duncan

Ellen, Petronella, Rebecca

<u>Miscellaneous 'PEACOCK' Bengal Baptisms (1862 ->)</u>:

Gertrude E.	1862	102	531

---

[256] OIOC (N/2/40/288).
[257] OIOC (N/2/42/201).

Eleanor B.	1865	111	343
Helen C.	1865	111	367
Henry B.	1866	118	16
George J.	1867	122	26

(the above up to and incl. 1867)

Miscellaneous 'PEACOCK' Madras Baptisms (1861 ->):

William H.C.	**1861**	**42**	**201**	**our William**
Ellen A.	1863	44	246	f. Henry Alexander, m. Adeline
Ernest H.S.	1865	46	12	f. Henry Alexander, m. Adeline
Ira M.L.	1866	47	242	
Emma M.R.	1867	48	202c/1	121f. Henry Alexander, m. Adeline
Emily	1867	48	259	f. Charles, m. Rachel
Thomas	1870	51	46	f. Jacob, m. Mary
John	1870	51	47	f. John, m. Michaela
Thomas G.	**1871**	**52**	**201**	**f. William George, m. Jane**

Ellen PEACOCK (née CAMPION) died between 1861 and 1867, though I have not been able to find a burial record at the OIOC.

William George PEACOCK remarried on 19 February 1868 to a 16 year old girl named Jane Anne Maria YOUNG, daughter of Richard Henry Long[258].

William and Jane had at least three children (not relations of mine):

PEACOCK, Rachel Maria Ellen (1869- ?) was born on 5 January 1869, and baptised at Chudderghaut on 5 March 1869. Her father was then 'Assistant to the Private Secretary, Nizam's Service'[259].

PEACOCK, Thomas George (1871- ?) was born on 4 July 1871, and baptised at Chudderghaut on 15 October 1871[260].

PEACOCK, Ella May (1880- ?) was born on 14 July 1880, and baptised on 5 November 1880 at Chudderghaut. Her father was then 'Head Asst to H.E. Private Secretary'.

b. Susannah CAMPION [1/2] (1843- ?) was born at Nagpur on 25 August 1843. The baptism record[261] states:

'At Nagpur; baptized: 26 November 1843; born: 25 August 1843; Susannah, girl, parents: Jeremiah & Ellen CAMPION; abode: Nagpore; father's occupation: Conductor of Ordnance; John McEvoy, (Chaplain).

---

[258] OIOC (N/2/49/294).

[259] OIOC (N/2/50/20).

[260] OIOC (N/2/52/201).

[261] OIOC (N/2/21/406).

We do not know whether Susannah died in infancy or married.

A Susannah CAMPION married in Northallerton in the Dec.1883 Quarter (9d, 1218), and another married in Liverpool in the Dec.1884 Quarter (8d, 264)[262].

There is no record of Susannah in the 1901 Census, possibly because the above Susannahs were not 'ours'.

c. Sarah Rebecca CAMPION [1/2] (1845-aft.1859) was born at Sitabuldi, near Nagpur, on 23 April 1845. The baptism record[263] states:

> *'Seetabuldi, Nagpore; baptized: 25 June 1845; born: 23 April 1845 (which I certify, J. Campion); Sarah Rebecca CAMPION, daughter of Jeremiah and Ellen CAMPION, of Seetabuldee, Nagpoor, Cond.of Ordnance, was baptized by me, John McEvoy, Chaplain, in the presence of J. H. Lynch, Rebekah Lynch, Sarah Whiteside'.*

We know that she was alive in 1859, aged about 14, because she was a witness at the baptism of her nephew, Henry PEACOCK (see above).

The Sarah Rebecca CAMPION who married at St Saviour, Southwark in April-June 1880 (1d,10) to John Robert DIGBY or Thomas WALLINGTON, is not ours (based on actual certificate).

d. Charlotte CAMPION [1/2] (1847-aft.1938) was baptised at Sitabuldi, near Nagpur, on 15 June 1847. The baptism record[264] states:

> *'Baptised: 29th September 1847; born: 15th June 1847 (I certify, G. R. Duncan); Charlotte, daughter of Jeremiah & Ellen CAMPION, of Seetabuldi, father's occupation: Conductor of Ordnance; abode: Nagpore; was baptized by me John McEvoy, in the presence of us: G. R. Duncan* [grandfather]*, M. Duncan* [step-grandmother]*, E. Campion* [mother]*'*

Peter Briscoe-Smith informed me that Mrs M.K. Briscoe-Smith said that Charlotte was born in Tipperary, Ireland and brought to India aged three months; she never returned to Ireland or England. It is technically possible that this happened, though the 2 ½ month gap between birth and baptism would have been hardly sufficient for the journey.

---

[262] Free BMDs.

[263] OIOC (N/2/24/117).

[264] OIOC (N/2/26/383).

Charlotte SMITH (née CAMPION)(1847-aft.1938) with her daughter Eva, and descendants

Charlotte married, on 16 October 1867 at Aurungabad, India, Henry Alexander Thomas SMITH (1846-1922), son of Henry Wilmot Smith[265]:

> *'Marriages solemnized at Aurungabad: 1867 Octr. 16; Henry Alexander Thomas SMITH; 21; Bachelor; Inspector of the Post Office, Berar District; res.: Akolah; father: Henry Wilmot Smith; and Charlotte CAMPION; 20; Spinster; abode: Aurungabad; father: Jeremiah Campion; by Licence; witnesses: J. Vital [?], M. Gannon[?], J. Campion [father of bride], H.W. Smith [father of groom]; Richard Firth, M.A., Chaplain'.*

Henry Smith became Deputy Postmaster-General in the Madras Government. He is reputed to have left Charlotte in India and set up house in England with a 'housekeeper'[266].

Charlotte and Henry had at least four children, listed below. There may have been other children 'in the gaps':

- before Henry (1868);

---

[265] OIOC (N/2/48/275).

[266] Peter Briscoe-Smith.

- between Henry and Eva (1870-71);

- between Frederick and Laura (1877-1888).

Because 'Smith' is such a common family name it would require searching virtually every microfilm in the relevant periods, and this will be done in time.

i) <u>Henry Wilmot SMITH</u> [2/1] (1869-1934), known as 'Harry', was 'discovered' by me on 2 August 2003. I was subsequently contacted (through Genes Reunited) by his great-grandson, Peter BRISCOE-SMITH (see below). Harry was born on 25 October 1869 and baptised five years later, probably in Sitabuldi, near Nagpur[267]:

> *'Baptisms solemnised at ....[illegible]: 25th October 1874; born: 25th October 1869; Henry Wilmot, Son of Henry & Charlotte SMITH; abode: Sitabuldi; occ.: Asst. to Chief Inspector of Post Office; David Whitlow [Chaplain?]'.*

There were no witnesses in the baptism record.

The following information comes from his obituary[268]: he was educated at Bishop Cotton School, Bangalore, and took the degree L.M.S. at Madras University. He came to England at the age of 20, obtaining an MB and CM at Edinburgh in 1896. He came to Darlastone in about 1899 and built up an extensive practice in The Green. He later joined a partnership with Dr G.I. Lamb, and was a member of Darlaston Council.

Henry Wilmot SMITH married Ada NORTON (1886-1944) on 28 December 1907 in Blackpool. They had two children:

> <u>Mary Kathleen SMITH</u> [3] (1909-1999), known as 'Kathleen', married (1938) Joseph Henry BRISCOE-SMITH (1913-1986), MB, ChB, DPH, LRCP, MRCS, son of John Alfred SMITH and Lily Annie BRISCOE. He joined the Indian Medical Service (IMS) and went to India in 1938, returning to England a year later, served in WW2 in the RAMC, and became Medical Officer of Health for the City of Westminster. They had two children:
>
> > <u>Elizabeth Anne BRISCOE-SMITH</u> [3/1] (b.1940), known as 'Liz', married the Rev. Louis Morton COULSON (b.1936).
> >
> > <u>Peter John BRISCOE-SMITH</u> [3/1] (b.1942), of Wimbledon, London[269], from whom I have obtained all the information about the descendants of Harry Wilmot Smith. He married

---

[267] OIOC (N/2/55/254).

[268] Obituary in Darlastone Newspapers (3 May 1934).

[269] Peter John Briscoe Smith, 150 Westway, Raynes Park, West Wimbledon, London SW20 9LS (tel: 020-8542-0505; peter@briscoe-smith.org.uk; <http://www.briscoe-smith.org.uk>.

Ann BALDWIN, and they have three children. Peter and Ann own properties in Raynes Park which they rent to visitors on a weekly basis:

> <u>Charles Peter BRISCOE-SMITH</u> [3/2] (b.1974), obtained a PhD at the U. of Kent.
> <u>Barbara Ann BRISCOE-SMITH</u> [3/2] (b.1976).
> <u>Margaret Louise   BRISCOE-SMITH</u> [3/2] (b.1976), twin of Barbara, married Benjamin WHITE. Barbara and Margaret have an event photography business.

<u>Harry Wilmot SMITH</u> [3] (1917-1967) was born in Darlaston married Phyllis …in 1936, served in WW2 and divorced in 1947. He had two children:

> <u>John SMITH</u> [3/1] (b.1938).
> <u>Jenifer SMITH</u> [3/1] (b.1943).

ii) <u>Eva Maria Charlotte SMITH</u> [2/1] (1872-aft.1904) was born on 16 March 1872 and baptised at Nagpur[270] on the same day as her brothers Henry (see above), and Frederick (see below):

> *'Baptisms solemnised at Nagpore: 25th October 1874; born: 16th March 1872; Eva Maria Charlotte, daughter of Henry and Charlotte SMITH; abode: Sitabuldi; occ.: Asst. to Chief Inspector of Post Office; David Whitlow [Chaplain?]'.*

Eva married (1st) on 24 October 1900, at Bangalore[271], Daniel J. KELLY (c.1875- ?), son of Patrick Kelly. Daniel was an Inspector in the Public Works Department.

> *'Marriages solemnised at St Patrick's Church, Bangalore: 1900 Oct.24; Daniel KELLY, 25, Bachelor; P.W.* [Public Works] *Inspector; abode: Khanapore; father: Patrick Kelly; Eva SMITH, 23, Spinster; abode: Bangalore; father: Henry Smith; by Licence;* [signed] *D.J. Kelly, E.M.C. Smith; witnesses: P.E. Kilroy, ……(illegible); Ant. M. Tabard, Chaplain'.*

Eva married (2nd) a Mr Maher.

Eva and Daniel KELLY had at least three children:

> <u>Carlton Campion Joseph KELLY</u> [3] (1901- ?) was born on 19 December 1901 and baptised on 11 January 1902 at St Patrick's Cathedral, Bangalore[272]:

---

[270] OIOC (N/2/55/254).

[271] OIOC (N/2/88/207).

[272] OIOC (N/2/91/65).

'Baptisms solemnised at St Patrick's Cathedral, Bangalore: 1902 Jan. 11; born: 1901 Dec. 19; Carlton Campion Joseph; male; parents: Daniel & Eva KELLY; abode: Khanapur; occ.: Permanent Way Inspector; Ant. M. Tabard (Priest)'.

<u>Doreen Charlotte Campion Mary KELLY</u> [3] (1903- ?) was born on 20 January 1903 and baptised on 13 February 1903 at St Patrick's Cathedral, Bangalore[273]:

'Baptisms solemnised at St Patrick's Cathedral, Bangalore: 1903 Feby. 13th; born 1903 Jany. 20th; Doreen Charlotte Campion Mary; female; parents: Daniel & Eva KELLY; abode: Khanapur; occ.: Permanent Way Inspector; Ant. M. Tabard (Priest)'.

<u>'Bonnie' KELLY</u> [3] married a Mr SHORTLAND

Or <u>'Queenie' KELLY</u> [3]

iii) <u>Frederick Russell SMITH</u> [2/1] (1873- ?) was 'discovered' by me in August 2003. He was born on 15 September 1873, and baptised together with his elder brother and sister on 25 October 1874[274]:

'Baptisms solemnised at Nagpore: 25th October 1874; born: 16th March 1872; Frederick Russell, son of Henry and Charlotte SMITH; abode: Sitabuldi; occ.: Asst. to Chief Inspector of Post Office; David Whitlow [Chaplain?]'.

There were no witnesses in the baptism record.

We do not know yet what happened to Frederick Russell SMITH.

iv) <u>Laura Ellen SMITH</u> [2/1] (1887-1969) was born on 22 March 1887 and baptised at Vepery, Madras, on 17 August 1888[275]:

'Baptisms solemnised at Vepery, Madras: 1888 August 17th; born: 1887 March 22; Laura Ellen, Female; parents: Henry & Charlotte SMITH; abode: Vepery; occ.: Superintendent of Post Office, Cocanada Division; W.H. Hobart, Chaplain of Vepery'.

Laura married on 6 December 1914, at the Wesleyan Church, St John's Hill, Bangalore, Randolph Robert SHELBY (1888-c.1945), son of John SHELBY[276]. He was a gunner in the RA, and later worked with the Madras Harbour Trust.

'Randolph Robert SHELBY, 26, Bachelor, Gunner R.P [or D]A.; abode: Bangalore; father: John Shelby; Laura Ellen SMITH, 26,

---

[273] OIOC (N/2/93/76).

[274] OIOC (N/2/55/254).

[275] OIOC (N/2/69/224).

[276] OIOC (N/2/116/216).

Spinster; abode: Bangalore; father: Henry Smith; witnesses: James Law, Lilian Bartells[?], signed: G.H. McCormick'.

Written at the top of the marriage certificate is: *Both European British Subjects.*

Laura Ellen and Randolph had six children (some may not be in correct order):

<u>Freda Irena SHELBY</u> [3] (1915) was born on 10 December 1915 and baptised on 24 December 1915 at St Martin's Church, Jhansi[277]:

> *'Baptisms solemnised at St Martin's, Jhansi: 1915 Dec.24; born: 1915 Dec. 10; Freda Irena; female; parents: Randolph Robert & Laura Ellen SHELBY; abode: Jhansi; occ.: Gunner 79th Batty. R.F.A.; N.R.O.G. Bennet, Chaplain'.*

Freda was (2002) in a nursing home in Cambridge. She married Ernest GRANT and had five daughters.

> <u>Katherine GRANT</u> [3/1] married (1st) Peter DOLPHIN, and (2nd) a Mr MARTIN, and had:
> > <u>Sarah Jane MARTIN</u> [3/2]
> > <u>Christopher MARTIN</u> [3/2]
> > <u>Stephen MARTIN</u> [3/2]
> > <u>Michael MARTIN</u> [3/2]
> > <u>Rachel MARTIN</u> [3/2]

> <u>Helen GRANT</u> [3/1]

> <u>Dawn GRANT</u> [3/1] (known as GRANT-TAYLOR) married a Mr TAYLOR, and had:
> > <u>Sean TAYLOR</u> [3/2] who married and had:
> > > <u>Lauren Charlotte TAYLOR</u> [3/3] (b.1997).

> <u>Barbara GRANT</u> [3/1]

> <u>Elizabeth GRANT</u> [3/1] married Kevin NAYLOR, and had:
> > <u>Hannah NAYLOR</u> [3/2]
> > <u>Zoe NAYLOR</u> [3/2]

<u>Sheilah SHELBY</u> [3] (c.1916–1956) married a Major BANDEEN.

<u>Randolph Garth SHELBY</u> [3] (1917-1998) was born on 24 July 1917 and baptised on 22 August 1922 at Kasauli[278]:

---

[277] OIOC (N/1/408/157).
[278] OIOC (N/1/422/129).

'Baptisms solemnised at Kasauli: 1917 August 22; born: 1917 July 24; Randolph Garth; son of Randolph Robert & Laura Ellen SHELBY; abode: Jullunder; occ.: Gunner, 79th Battery, R.F.A.; B. Saunders Dyer, Chaplain'.

He attended the Lawrence Memorial Royal Military School, where he was Drum Major. He joined the Northamptonshire Regiment in India, and went to England soon after WW2. He married Edith Rosa TAVERNOR and had seven children:

Edith Elizabeth SHELBY [3/1] married Tony POYNTON and had:

Adrian POYNTON [3/2]

Randolph Gordon SHELBY [3/1] known as 'Gordon' married Gillian BURDETT [393 Stanton Road, Burton-on-Trent, Staffs. Tel: 01283-511862]. They had:

Susan SHELBY [3/2] married Laurence WARD, and had:
Lauren WARD [3/3]
Rosalyn WARD [3/3]
Claire WARD [3/3]
Kim WARD [3/3]

Sheila Joyce SHELBY [3/1] married Alan BOOTH, and had:
Philip BOOTH [3/2]
Martin BOOTH [3/2]

Colleen Mary SHELBY [3/1] married Graham KIDD and had:
Michael KIDD [3/2]
Katy KIDD [3/2]

Brian Garth SHELBY [3/1] married Sarah MASSINGHAM and had:
Rebecca SHELBY [3/2]

Eleanor SHELBY [3/2]

Melanie June SHELBY [3/1] married Roy Van BARRETT and had:
Myles BARRETT [3/2]
Grace BARRETT [3/2]

Doreen Rosa SHELBY [3/1] married Roy WILLIAMS [44 Maxstoke Road, Sutton Coldfield, B73 5OR; tel: 01216-043326]. They had:
Amie WILLIAMS [3/2]
Russell WILLIAMS [3/2]

Lewis WILLIAMS [3/2]

John Reginald SHELBY [3] (b.c.1918-1919).

Doreen Joyce SHELBY [3] (b.1920) was born on 31 July 1920 and baptised on 15 August 1920 at St Mary's Church, Pune (Poona)[279]:

> *'Baptisms solemnised in St Mary's Church, Poona: 1920 Aug.15; born: 1920 July 31; Doreen Joyce; female; parents: Randolph Robert & Laura Helen [sic] SHELBY; abode: Jullunder; occ.: Gunner, R.F.A.; H. Ll. Arnould, Chaplain'.*

She married (1945) Benjamin SELLAR, and had three children:

> Gordon SELLAR [3/1] (b.1946) lives in Perth, WA [Unit 4, 40-42 Hopkinson Way, Wilson, WA 6107, Australia; tel: 61-8-9356-3724].

> Gillian Esther SELLAR [3/1] (b.1951) married Tony RANSOME. She lives in Denmark, WA, south of Perth [Tel: Denmark: 61-8-9848-1865; Perth: 61-8-9458-2307]

> They had:

>> Ocea RANSOME [3/2] (b.1983).

> Stuart Benjamin SELLAR [3/1] (b.1955) married (1984) Cheryl PALEY, and had:
>> Joshua SELLAR [3/2] (b.1986).
>> Kate Louise SELLAR [3/2] (b.1989).

Gladys Audrey SHELBY [3] (1922) was born on 28 July 1922 and baptised on 15 August 1922 at Holy Trinity Church, St John's, Bangalore[280]:

> *'Baptisms solemnised at Holy Trinity, St John's, Bangalore: 1922 Augst.15th; born: 1922 July 28; Gladys Audrey; daughter of Randolph Robert & Laura Ella [sic] SHELBY; abode: Bangalore; occ.: Gunner 5th Amm. Column, R.F.A.; E.O. Jervis, M.A., Chaplain'.*

Gladys married John HARRIS and had two children[281]:

> Geoffrey HARRIS [3/1] married Jill, and had:

---

[279] OIOC (N/3/124/53).
[280] OIOC (N/2/132/3).
[281] Pers.comm.: Gordon Sellar.

Bradley HARRIS [3/2]

Rebecca HARRIS [3/2] now living in Adelaide, S. Australia.

Christina HARRIS [3/1] married Glen CAMERON and had:

Craig CAMERON [3/2]

Sarah CAMERON [3/2]

Peter Briscoe-Smith lists two additional children:

v) Dorry SMITH [2/1] who married Alfred STEWART-JACKS and had four children:

unknown STEWART-JACKS [3]

Harry STEWART-JACKS [3]

Vincent STEWART-JACKS [3]

Irene STEWART-JACKS [3]

vi) Ida SMITH [2/1] who married Spencer MOLLAN, known as 'Burt'. Note that Ida and Burt attended the funeral of Ida's brother, Henry Wilmot SMITH in 1934 in Darlaston, England. Ida and Burt had four children[282]:

Dennis MOLLAN [3] who married Kathleen WHISTANCE, and had a daughter:

Diane MOLLAN [3/1] who was a train-bearer at the wedding of Peter Briscoe-Smith's mother's wedding (in 1938).

Terence Edward Dermott MOLLAN [3]

Colleen MOLLAN [3]

Molly MOLLAN [3] who married Walter HALES, a policeman. They had a son:

David HALES [3/1]

e. Henry CAMPION [1/2] (1849-aft.1873) was born at Sitabuldi, near Nagpur, on 18 April 1849. The baptism record[283] states:

'Baptised: 31ˢᵗ October 1849; born: 18ᵗʰ April 1849 (which I certify, J. Campion); Henry, son of Jeremiah & Ellen CAMPION, of Seetabuldee, Nagpore; father's occupation: Conductor of Ordnance; was baptized by me John McEvoy, M.A., in the presence of us: T(?). Abercrombie, J. Campion [father], *A. W. Campion'.*

'A.W. Campion' is Anne Wilhelmina CAMPION (1835-1866).

---

[282] E-mail from Peter Briscoe-Smith (11 Feb 2006)

[283] OIOC (N/2/28/539).

We know little of what happened to Henry. There is no record of him in the 1881 and 1901 Censuses. However, he evidently contested the inheritance of Leitrim House by his half-brother Jeremiah CAMPION II (1829-1877) on the death of their father in 1871. The trial proceedings were reported in the Cork Examiner of 28 March 1872, and I have seen a copy in the possession of June and Michael Hews[284]. The case was at the Cork Spring Assizes (Jeremiah Campion vs. Henry Campion). At the trial, Henry agreed to the legitimacy of his half-brother Jeremiah, and they divided the estate equally so as not 'to waste the entire property in litigation'. Jeremy [Jeremiah] conveyed a portion of the estate to Henry by deed, dated 28 April 1873.

f. <u>George Roan Duncan CAMPION</u> [1/2] (1851-1851) was born on 2 January 1851 at Mhow, Bengal. The baptism record[285] states:

> '*Baptisms solemnized at Mhow in the Archdeaconry and Diocese of Calcutta. Baptized: 1851 February 5th; born: 1851 January 2nd; George Rowen [sic] Duncan, son of Jeremiah and Ellen CAMPION; abode: Mhow; father's occupation: Conductor of Ordnance; C.W. Cahusac, Chaplain*'.

George died eight months later, on 1 September 1851, and was buried at Mhow; the burial record[286] states:

> '*Burials at Mhow in the deaconry & Diocese of Calcutta: 1851 Sept. 1st George Rowen Duncan CAMPION; 8 months; son of Conductor Campion, Ordnance Department; bu. September 1st; C.W. Cahusac(?), Chaplain*'.

Note that a Jeremiah CAMPION married at Shillong (Assam) in 1904[287]:

> '*Marriages solemnised at the Catholic Church, Shillong: 1904 Decr. 14; Jeremiah CAMPION, 39, Bachelor, Soldier, abode: Shillong; father: William Campion; Mary O'SHEA, 37, widow, abode: Chotijau[?]; father: John Ryan; witnesses: H.J. Lawrie, E.J. Hibbert; G. Schoeb, S.D.S.*'.

William Campion (this Jeremiah's father) might have been the brother of 'our' Jeremiah, assuming he married in about 1864, and was born in about 1840.

---

[284] June and Michael HEWS [14 Oakdene, Lansdown Road, Cheltenham, GL5 16PX (tel: 01242-260905)].

[285] OIOC (N/1/79/64).

[286] OIOC (N/1/80/189).

[287] OIOC (N/1/321/39).

APPENDIX D: THE THIPTHORPS AND DE LA HOYDES

1. <u>Mary Faith Olivia DE LA HOYDE</u> [1/2] (1877-aft.1912) was born on 10 May 1877 and baptised at Dalhousie, Punjab. The Raincock family tree has her first name as 'May'. Her baptism record[288] states:

> *'Baptisms solemnized at Dalhousie: 1877 June 8th; born: 1877 May 10th; Mary Faith Olivia, daughter of George & Mary Faith DE LA HOYDE; abode: Dalhousie; father's occ: Accountant P.W.D; J. R. Lewin, Minister'.*

The name 'Olivia' probably honours the child's great-grandmother, Olivia DE LA HOYDE (née PRITCHARD)(1811-1939). She is mentioned in a letter from David Dinwiddie[289]: *"George Dela Hoyde [sic] is married to the youngest Miss Duncan; has a Baby girl and doing nicely in a hill station called Dalhousie".*

She married William Henry THIPTHORP (bef.1878-aft.1918), an Assistant Surgeon in the Indian Medical Service (IMS) in Jabalpore, on 4 October 1899. We know he lived until 1935, because he was a witness at the wedding of Millicent DE LA HOYDE in that year. He was the son of Charles Thipthorp, whose wife was Theodosia Mabel THEOBALD[290] (they married in 1863, Madras Presidency)[291]. Charles and Theodosia had other children: Catherine Lavinia Mabel (b.1864[292]), Florence Augusta (b.1872; bap.1873 at Sitabuldi[293]) who was Neville Tyler's grandmother, Ernest Ebenezer (b.1876, Wardah, W.Bengal)[294]. Florence Augusta THIPTHORPE married Herbert Walter Ritchie TYLER in Nagpur on 27 February 1901[295].

William is not listed in Crawford's 'Roll of the I.M.S.', presumably because he was a mere <u>Assistant</u> Surgeon. It is unclear whether the family name is spelt THIPTHORP or THIPTHORPE. I have used the latter, because the baptism of all three (known) children is spelled with the 'E' at the end of the name (see below).

The marriage record[296], which has the original signatures, states:

> *'4 October 1899; William Henry THIPTHORP; age: full; Bachelor; Asst. Surgeon, IMS; abode: Alipore, Calcutta; father: Charles Thipthorp; and Mary Faith Olivia DE LA HOYDE; age: full; spinster; abode: Jabalpore, C.P.* [Central Provinces], *father: George de la Hoyde; married in the Wesleyan Church, Jabalpore; witnesses: George de la Hoyde, Herbert Leonard Thipthorp'.*

---

[288] OIOC (N/1/160/20).

[289] DD letter to his sisters Margaret & Janet (10-26.12.1877).

[290] Madras marriage (1863): N/2/44/195.

[291] OIOC (N/2/44/195) from Neville Tyler (19.2.2005).

[292] IGI: Batch C750197.

[293] OIOC (N/1/143/59).

[294] E-mail from Neville Tyler (19.2.2005) Neville.tyler@virgin.net.

[295] E-mail from Neville Tyler (19.2.2005).

[296] OIOC (N/1/regr./1149/00) (N/11/9/c33).

Mary and William had at least three children. However, the gaps in 1900-1902, 1904-1906, and 1908-1911, suggest that other children might have been born:

a) <u>Dorothea Mabel THIPTHORPE</u> [2/1] (c.1900-aft.1918) was 'discovered' by me in June 2004. I have not yet found her baptism record.

She was married, on 12 June 1918 at Murree, to John Reid HEPPOLETTE[297]:

> *'Marriages solemnised at Murree: 1918 June 12; John Reid HEPPOLETTE; age: full; Bachelor; occ. Assistant Surgeon, I.S.M.D., abode: Murree; Dorothe [sic] Mabel THIPTHORP, 18, Spinster, abode: Murree, father: William Henry Thipthorp; Banns; witnesses: Chas Dyer, W.H. Thipthorp [father]; T.H. Dixon, Chaplain'.*

b) <u>Doris May THIPTHORPE</u> [2/1] (1903- ?) was born on 28 October 1903 and baptised at Meerut[298]:

> *'Baptisms solemnised at St John's Church, Meerut: 1903 Decr. 14th; born 1903 October 28th; Doris May, daughter of William Henry & Mary Olivia THIPTHORPE [sic]; abode: Meerut; Assistant Surgeon, I.M.S; Walter Kitchin, Chaplain'.*

c) <u>Freda Dulcie THIPTHORPE</u> [2/1] (1907- ?) was born on 15 February 1907[299]:

> *'1907 March 29th, Good Friday; born: 1907 Feby. 15th; Freda Dulcie; daughter of William Henry & Mary Faith THIBTHORPE [sic]; abode: Meerut; Assistant Surgeon, I.S.M. [sic]; W.C. Granville Sharp, Chaplain'.*

Freda married Norman PRIDEAUX. I have no information about children.

d) <u>Theodore Henry THIPTHORPE</u> [2/1] (1912- ?) was born on 24 July 1912 and baptised at Howrah[300]:

> *'Baptisms solemnized at St Thomas' Church, Howrah: 1912 Sept. 29th; born: 1912 July 24th; Theodore Harry, son of William Henry & Mary Faith THIPTHORPE, abode: Paksey Sarah [?]; occ.: Asst. Surgeon; A.C. Ridsdale, Chaplain'.*

This entry is crossed through and *'amended see above'* written over it, and a date: *'27.6.31'* – could this be a marriage date? The revised entry changes the second name from 'Harry' to 'Henry'.

2. <u>Hugh Duncan DE LA HOYDE</u> [1/2] (1879-1914) was born on 23 January 1879 and baptised at Dalhousie, Bengal. His baptism record[301] states:

> *'Baptisms solemnized at Dalhousie: 1879 February 16th; born: 1879 January 23rd; Hugh Duncan, son of George & Mary Faith DE LA HOYDE; abode: Dalhousie; father's occ: Accountant P.W.D; J. R. Lewin, Minister'.*

---

[297] OIOC (N/1/429/381).

[298] OIOC (N/1/312/107).

[299] OIOC (N/1/338/108).

[300] OIOC (N/1/384/23).

[301] OIOC (N/1/167/21).

The Raincock tree has him as the first child. 'Hugh' and 'Duncan' are both family names, but it's rather surprising that the first boy was not named 'George' or 'Christopher'. According to the Raincock tree, he died without issue.

3. <u>Emily DE LA HOYDE</u> [1/2] (1880- ?), known as 'Amy', was born on 10 October 1880 and baptised at Dalhousie, Punjab. Her baptismal record[302] states:

> *'Baptism solemnized at Dalhousie; 1880 Oct. 27th; born: 1880 Oct. 10th, Emily, daughter of George and Mary Faith DE LA HOYDE; abode: Dalhousie; occ: Accountant P.W.D; J. R. Lewin, Chaplain'.*

> Emily did not marry, and lived in retirement at Newton Abbott, Devon.

4. <u>Bridget Lydia DE LA HOYDE</u> [1/2] (1882- ?) was born on 9 December 1882 and baptised at Dalhousie. She was 'discovered' by me on 15 October 2001. Her baptism record[303] states:

> *'Baptism solemnized at Dalhousie; 1883 January 1883; born: 1883 [sic] December 9th, Bridget Lydia, daughter of George and Mary Faith DE LA HOYDE; abode: Dalhousie; occ: Accountant P.W.D; J. R. Lewin, Chaplain of Dalhousie'.*

The name 'Lydia' presumably honours the child's aunt, Lydia Rebecca DUNCAN (1850-1922). Her absence from the 'Raincock tree' might be because she died in infancy.

5. <u>George Duncan Nevill (or Nowell) DE LA HOYDE</u> [1/2] was born on 21 April 1887 and baptised at Sitabuldi[304]:

> *'Baptisms solemnized at All Saints Church, Seetabuldee: 1887 May 20th; born: 1887 April 21st; George Duncan Nevill, son of George and Mary Faith DE LA HYDE [sic], Morar; occ: accountant, PWD; F.D. Gray, Chaplain'.*

Although his third name was spelt 'Nevill' in his baptism record, it is spelt 'Nowell' in his marriage record, and in the baptism records of his children. He became a boiler maker (marriage record, 1915), and later a workshop foreman in the Bengal Nagpur Railway (son's baptism record, 1927).

He married Dorothy EDWARDS (c.1893-aft.1920), daughter of John Edwards, on 22 December 1915[305] at Khargpur, Bengal:

> *'Marriages solemnised at Khargpur: George Duncan Nowell [sic] DE LA HOYDE, 28, bachelor, Boiler Maker, abode: Adra; father: George De La Hoyde; & Dorothy EDWARDS, 22, spinster, abode: Khargpur; father: John Edwards; by banns; witnesses: William R. Malcolm, John Edwards; G. Reynold Walters, Chaplain'.*

---

[302] OIOC (N/1/174/21).

[303] OIOC (N/1/183/49).

[304] OIOC (N/1/200/33).

[305] OIOC (N/1/409/388).

They had at least four children:

a) <u>Duncan Edward DE LA HOYDE</u> **2/1** (1916) was born on 29 October 1916 and baptised on 12 November 1916 at Khargpur, Bengal, India[306]:

> *'Baptisms solemnised at Khargpur: 1916 November 12; born: 1916 October 1916; Duncan Edward, son of George Duncan Nowell & Dorothy DE LA HOYDE; abode: Adra; occ.: District Boiler Maker, B.N. Ry.* [Bengal Nagpur Railway]*; T.A. Thomson, Chaplain of Cuttack'.*

He married Stella ....and had a son (Richard). After Duncan died, Stella and her son moved to South Africa.

<u>Richard DE LA HOYDE</u> 3

b) <u>Freda Constance Beatrice DE LA HOYDE</u> **2/1** (1918-1960) was born on 19 February 1918 and baptised on 10 March 1918 at Adra, Bengal, India[307]:

> *'Baptisms solemnised at Adra, B.N.* [Bengal Nagpur] *Railway: 1918 March 10; born: 1918 February 19; Freda Constance Beatrice, daughter of George Duncan Nowell & Dorothy DE LA HOYDE; abode: Nagpur; occ: Forman, B.N.Ry* [Bengal Nagpur Railway] *Workshop; R.G. Ledgard, Archdeacon'.*

Freda kept house for her father George after his wife Dorothy died. She did not marry.

c) <u>Dorothy Maud DE LA HOYDE</u> **2/1** (1920- ?) was born on 30 April 1920 and baptised on 14 May 1920 at All Saints Church, Kharagpur, Bengal, India[308]:

> *'Return of baptisms at All Saints Church, Khargpur: 1920 May 14th; born: 1920 April 30th; Dorothy Maud, daughter of George & Dorothy DE LA HOYDE; abode: Khargpur; occ.: Asst. Foreman; Russel Payne, Chaplain of Khargpur'.*

She married, and had a son:

<u>Richard ....</u> 3

d) <u>Clifford DE LA HOYDE</u> **2/1** (1927- ?) was born on 29 October 1927, and was baptised on the same day in All Saints Church, Nagpur[309]. He was 'discovered' by me in August 2003:

> *'Baptisms solemnised at All Saints Church, Nagpore: 1927 Oct.29; born: 1927 Oct.29; Clifford; male; parents: George Duncan Nowell & Dorothy DE LA HOYDE; abode: Nagpur; occ: Forman, B.N.Ry* [Bengal Nagpur Railway] *Workshop; R.G. Ledgard, Archdeacon'.*

---

[306] OIOC (N/1/416/155).

[307] OIOC (N/1/426/46).

[308] OIOC (N/1/444/258).

[309] OIOC (N/1/504/160).

6. <u>Alice DE LA HOYDE</u> [1/2] (1889-1889) was born on 25 March 1889 and baptised at Sitabuldi. She was 'discovered' by me on 15 October 2001. Her baptism record[310] states:

> *'Baptisms solemnised at All Saints Church, Sitabuldi; 1889 April 22nd; born: 1889 March 25th; Alice, daughter of George & Mary Faith DE LA HOYDE; abode: Nagpur; occ: Accountant P. W. D; A. G. A. Roberts, Chaplain'.*

Alice died of smallpox in infancy on 10 May 1889; the burial record[311] states:

> *'Burials at Sitabuldee, Nagpur: 1889 May 10th; Alice de la Hoyde; age: 1 month 15 days; Infant daughter of Geo. De la Hoyde, Acct. PWD; buried: 1889 May 10th; cause: Smallpox; A.G.A. Roberts, Chaplain',*

I presume the burial was in All Saints Cathedral, Sitabuldi.

7. <u>Christopher Read Duncan DE LA HOYDE III</u> [1/2] (1890- ?) was born on 16 June 1890 and baptised at Sitabuldi, near Nagpur. His baptism record[312] states:

> *'All Saints Church, Sitabuldi; 1890 July 9th; born: 1890 June 16th; Christopher Read Duncan, son of George & Mary Faith DE LA HOYDE; abode: Nagpur; occ: Accountant P. W. D; A. G. A. Roberts, Chaplain'.*

He was a driver (loco?) on a railway (BNR?). He married (1st), perhaps about 1915, Irene MacLEAN, who was born in Nairobi, Kenya. He married (2nd) Vida Alexander (or Alexandra) HUNTLEY and had seven children:

a) <u>Ena Mavis DE LA HOYDE</u> [2/1] was was born on 12 April 1922 and baptised at St George's Church, Jamshedpur, on 2 May 1922[313]:

> *'Baptisms solemnised at St George's Church, Jamshedpur: 1922 May 2; born: 1922 April 12; Ena Mavis, daughter of Christopher Reid [sic] & Vida Alexander [sic] DELABOYDE [sic]; No.4 Loco-Quarters; abode: Sandragachi[?]; occ.: Engine Driver; ....Brighton [Minister]'.*

She married John NORRIS and had eleven children, probably born in the 1940s or 1950s:

<u>Roland NORRIS</u> [3]
<u>Tangi NORRIS</u> [3]
<u>Michael NORRIS</u> [3]
<u>Christine NORRIS</u> [3]
<u>Peter NORRIS</u> [3]
<u>Georgina NORRIS</u> [3]
<u>Christopher NORRIS</u> [3]
<u>Eleanor NORRIS</u> [3]
<u>Margaret NORRIS</u> [3]

---

[310] OIOC (N/1/208/158).
[311] OIOC (N/1/208/538).
[312] OIOC (N/1/213/92).
[313] OIOC (N/1/460/153).

<u>Leslie NORRIS</u> [3]
<u>Maria NORRIS</u> [3]

b) <u>David DE LA HOYDE</u> [2/1] (b.1924) was born on 18 October 1924 and baptised at Chakradharpur[314]:

> *'Baptisms solemnised at Chakradharpur: 1924 Novr 8; 1924 Oct 18; David Reid [sic], Male, parents: Christopher – Vida Alexander DE LA HOYDE; abode: Chakradhapur; occ.: Driver; Rev. G. Verloove'.*

He married Pauline, and had a daughter:

<u>Wendy DE LA HOYDE</u> [3]

c) <u>Lavinia (Lovina?) Primrose DE LA HOYDE</u> [2/1] (b.1926) was born on 26 November 1926 and baptised in Jamshedpur[315]:

> *'Return of baptisms, Catholic Church, Jamshedpur: 1928 Oct. 4; born: 1926 Nov.26; Lovina[?] Primrose; parents: Christopher Reid & Vida Alexander DE LA HOYDE, Chakradapur; occ.: driver; Rev. G. Verlove, R.C. Chaplain'.*

She was baptised again on 2 January 1944 at Jamshedpur, with her siblings Cynthia Mary and.George Duncan DE LA HOYDE[316]. She married (1st) William BARRY, and (2nd) John HALLORAN.

d) <u>Cynthia Mary DE LA HOYDE</u> [2/1] (b.1928) was born on 11 September 1928 and baptised in Jamshedpur[317]:

> *'Return of baptisms at Jamshedpur: 1944 January 2; born: 11 September 1928; Cynthia Mary, daughter of Christopher Reid and Veda Alexandra [sic] DE LA HOYDE; abode: Jamshedpur; occ.: Driver T. I. S. Co.; T.H. Page, Chaplain'.*

She married Thomas DANKS and had a son:

<u>Leonard Christopher DANKS</u> [3]

e) <u>Terence DE LA HOYDE</u> [2/1]

f) <u>Pamela DE LA HOYDE</u> [2/1] married Roland WOOD

---

[314] OIOC (N/1/480/83).

[315] OIOC (N/1/512/77).

[316] OIOC (N/1/622/11).

[317] OIOC (N/1/512/77 & N/1/622/11).

They had four children:
> Sandra WOOD [3]
> Philip WOOD [3]
> Charmaine WOOD [3]
> Carol WOOD [3]

g) <u>George Duncan DE LA HOYDE</u> [2/1] (b.1938) was born on 29 March 1938, and baptised in Jamshedpur[318]:

> *'Return of baptisms at Jamshedpur: 1944 January 2; born: 29 March 1938; George Duncan, son of Christopher Reid and Veda Alexandra [sic] DE LA HOYDE; abode: Jamshedpur; occ.: Driver T. I. S. Co.; T.H. Page, Chaplain'.*

He married Peta HURST and had three children:

i) <u>Christopher DE LA HOYDE</u> [3] married Deborah BARDOE and had two children:
> Cara DE LA HOYDE [3/1]
> Louis DE LA HOYDE [3/1]

ii) <u>Alison DE LA HOYDE</u> [3] married Martin COOPER and had a son:

> Joel COOPER [3/1]

iii) <u>Jeremy DE LA HOYDE</u> [3] married Joanne COX and had three children:
> Amy DE LA HOYDE [3/1]
> Daniel DE LA HOYDE [3/1]
> Leah DE LA HOYDE [3/1]

8. <u>Freda DE LA HOYDE</u> [1/2] (1892-1960) was born on 20 February 1892, and baptised at Sitabuldi[319]:

> *'Baptisms solemnized at All Saints Church, Sitabuldi: 1892 March 9th; born: 1892 February 20th; Freda, daughter of George and Mary Faith DE LA HOYDE; abode: Nagpur; occ: Accountant, PWD; Arthur Charles Pearson, Chaplain'.*

9. <u>Millicent Dorothy DE LA HOYDE</u> [1/2] (1894-1932) was born on 12 March 1894, and baptised in Nagpur[320]:

> *'C.of E. returns Central Provinces: 1894 April 10th; born: 1894 March 12th; Dorothy Milicent [sic], Female; parents: George and Mary Faith DE LA HOYDE; abode: Nagpur; occ: Accountant, Public Works Department; C.H. Barlow, Chaplain'.*

Millicent married, on 30 September 1918 at Lahore, Ernest Albert B.... PHILIPPE (c.1888- ?), son of Arthur Philippe[321]:

---

[318] OIOC (N/1/512/77 & N/1/622/11).

[319] OIOC (N/1/219/172).

[320] OIOC (N/1/237/132).

[321] OIOC (N/1/431/15).

'Marriages solemnized at Lahore[?]: 1918 Sept. 30th; Ernest Albert B.....[?], PHILIPPE; 30; Bachelor; Sergeant, R.A.F.; abode: Lahore[?]; father: Arthur Philippe; and Millicent Dorothy DE LA HOYDE; 24; Spinster; Lahore[?]; father: George De La Hoyde; by Banns; witnesses: W.H. Thipthorpe [sic], Asst. Surgeon, James Bertie Law[?], E. de la Hoyde; Harold K.....[?], Chaplain'.

Parts of the above entry are difficult to read. The witness 'W.H. Thipthorpe' is William Henry Thipthorp, brother-in-law of the bride; and 'E. de la Hoyde' is probably Emily De La Hoyde, sister of the bride.

Millicent and Ernest had (at least) a son:

    a) <u>Ernest George Albert PHILIPPE</u> **2/1** known as 'Phil'[322], who has corresponded (2001) with Denys De La Hoyde.

After Mary Faith's death, George DE LA HOYDE married (2nd, 1899) Lilian BURKE and had four children (see Chapter 3: The Family of George De La Hoyde in THE PRITCHARDS AND MACKENZIES).

---

[322] <egphil@farebase.net>

APPENDIX E: THE GILMORE-FOSTER FAMILY.

My connection with the GILMORE-FOSTER family comes through the marriage of my great-aunt Mary Emily DUNCAN (1876-1924) to Walter Gelston GILMORE. Mary was the daughter of my great-grandparents **George Roan DUNCAN II** (1853-1901) and **Mary Jane DINWIDDIE** (1848-1918).

I am indebted to Chris Wheeler my 2nd cousin (see below) who gave me much of the information in this chapter. He in turn took a lot from the memoirs of Esmond FOSTER. Their children, Jeremy Foster and Meriel Comerford, have also contributed much material. It would be interesting if family members could add more detail, and even better if we could meet! I have always regarded the Fosters as 'family'. We spent time together in Kharagpur, Calcutta and Colombo during our childhood. Our paths crossed again in Northern and Southern Rhodesia. Alas, we have seen each other only intermittently since then.

Mary Emily DUNCAN[GA] (1876-1924) was born on 13 October 1876, and baptised at Sitabuldi (near Nagpur). The baptism record[323] states:

> *'Baptisms solemnized at All Saints Church, Sitabuldi: 1876 Oct. 31st; born: 1876 Oct.13th; Mary Emily DUNCAN; dr of George Roan and Mary Jane DUNCAN, abode: Kamthi; Accountant PWD; A.H. Etty(?), Chaplain'.*

Her grandfather David DINWIDDIE wrote:*"My daughter gave birth to a fine healthy girl on the 13th Oct. last, so I am a grandfather for the first time"[324]*. As George and Jane were living near the Dinwiddies in Kamptee, David Dinwiddie mentions his granddaughter several times: *"Your former correspondent Jane, has now a baby to care for, a fine plump healthy Daughter, now about 3 months old"[325]. "...Mrs Duncan with her guide man and little girl Mary live close by our house here in Kamptee. I think I could walk to their bungalow in about 3 minutes. Their little Mary is now about 14 months old and toddling...".*

Esmond Lewis Pearce FOSTER (her son in law) wrote of her: *'She was very unfit and her heart was in a hopeless mess even then. She must have been a good looking woman, but I never saw early photos of her, but, by that time, eternal hot weathers, a large family and inability to find money to go away for a change had burnt out any beauty there may have been. I think that it is very probable that the only time she left the plains of India was in 1914 when they took the children home (i.e., to England) to school. What the hot weather failed to destroy, was her infinite kindness and sweetness, and that is why everyone wanted to talk to her by the hour. She had a beautiful singing voice and was an able pianist. She had a low, rather husky speaking voice which was very attractive: in voice there was a distinct resemblance between her and her young brother, Houston DUNCAN. She died singing, with Mummy (Norah Estelle GILMORE) sitting beside her bed.'*

Before Mary died, she and her husband Walter were building Gelston House into which they intended to retire. She died before it could be finished. Felicity Pearce FOSTER (see below) was born in Gelston House. During the war, it became the Divisional Headquarters of the Jungle Warfare Training School in

---

[323] OIOC (N/1/158/40).

[324] David Dinwiddie to Margaret and Janet, 3 Jan.1876.

[325] David Dinwiddie to Janet Fergusson, 27 Jan.1877.

which the Chindits were trained. Mary and her husband lie in Chhindwara Cemetary, almost in sight of the house where Norah Estelle GILMORE was born.

Mary's burial record[326] states:

> '*Burials at Chhindwara; 1924 May 22; Mary GILMORE; 47 years; Wife of Mr W.G. GILMORE, Deputy Conservator of Forests; buried: 1924 May 23rd; cause of death: Heart Failure; Aug. Furlong, Missionary*'.

Mary Emily married in Nagpur in 1897. The marriage record[327] states:

> '*Marriages solemnized at All Saints Church, Nagpur; 1897 January 20; Walter Gelston GILMORE; age: full; Bachelor; Forest Department; abode: Bhandara(?); father: Charles GILMORE; Mary Emily DUNCAN, age: 20; Spinster; abode: Nagpur; father: George Roan DUNCAN; witnesses: R. Dinwiddie, A.R. Hunt, G. Duncan; C.H. Barlow, Chaplain*'.

Marriage of Mary Emily DUNCAN (1876-1924) and Walter Gelston GILMORE, at Nagpur, India, on 20 January 1897

---

[326] OIOC (N/1/477/199).

[327] OIOC (N/1/256/70).

Mary's husband, Walter Gelston GILMORE was in the Indian Forestry Service. He was the son of Charles(?) Denis GILMORE (Artillery) and Jane BANN[328]. He entered the Central Provinces Forest Service via the Ranger College, Dehra Dun, and became Extra Assistant Conservator, probably in 1894. One of his first jobs was the demarcation of the famous Alapilli Reserve in South Chanda division probably in or about 1896, or earlier. In about 1921 he was promoted to Deputy Conservator of Forests and transferred to the Seoni Division. He retired in or about 1923 as a result of quarrels with his Conservator. They hated each other and the remarks he made about his senior officer were intemperate to say the least. Had he behaved more reasonably, he would have been promoted to Conservator as he was a fine forest officer with a vast knowledge of India, her forests and people. He lies buried in the Chhindwara cemetery, within a mile of the house where Norah Estelle GILMORE was born.

Mary and Walter had five children, one of whom was reputed to have died in infancy of cholera in 1898:

1. Oliver(?) GILMORE [1/1] (1898-1900?) was born on 11 August 1898 at *'Wavangal, Nizam's Dominions, the wife of W.G. Gilmore, Assistant Conservator of Forests, H.H.N.D., of a son* [329]. I have not yet been able to find a baptism or burial record for this child. Meriel Comerford (see below) says his name was Oliver, and that he died of cholera at the age of two[330].

2. Eileen Gelston Duncan GILMORE [1/1] (1900- ?) was born in India in 1900, according to Meriel Comerford. I have not yet been able to find her baptism record.

   She was great fun, was Aunt Eileen, and a born - and probably frustrated - great actress, and in her youth must have been stunningly lovely, and she had all the assurance in the wide world [331].

   She married, at Raipur, India, on 26 January 1921, Herbert Jasper BELL (c.1887- ?), known as 'Jasper'. The marriage record[332] states:

   'Marriages solemnised at Raipur, C.P.: 1921 Jany. 26th; Herbert Jasper BELL; 34; Bachelor; Executive Engineer, P.W.D.; res.: Jubbulpore; father: Hubert Mande Bell; Eileen Gelston Duncan GILMORE; 20; Spinster; res.: Raipur; father: Walter Gelston Gilmore; Banns; witnesses: M.G. Gilmore; G.W. Benton[?]; A.F.G. Wardell, Chaplain, Jubbulpore'.

   Just before Eileen and her family went to Kenya, at Christmas 1932, there was a big family gathering at Esmond and Norah FOSTERS's home (see below), when Eileen was determined to shoot a tiger. Betty Duncan recollects that Esmond organised a beat, Eileen wounded the tiger, and it was never found. Jasper later worked in Germany, while the family lived in Beckenham [13 Hayne Road, Beckenham, Kent[333]].

   They had six children, and emigrated from India to Kenya before WW2.

---

[328] E-mail from Chris Wheeler (Aug.2001).

[329] *'The Friend of India'*, 25.8.1898.

[330] e-mail dated 12.8.2002.

[331] Meriel Comerford: e-mail (6.9.02).

[332] OIOC (N/1/451/191).

[333] Betty Duncan's address book.

a. <u>Doreen Joy Maude BELL</u> **²** (1921- ?) was born on 29 November 1921, and was baptised at Jabalpur on 24 February 1922[334]:

> *'Baptisms solemnised at Christ Church, Jubbulpore: 1922 February 24th; born: 1921 November 29th; Doreen Joy Maude, daughter of Herbert Jasper and Eileen Gelston Duncan BELL; abode: Jubbulpore, C.P.; father's occ.: Executive Engineer, PWD; A.F.G. Wardell, Chaplain'.*

> *'Doreen....has been married – I think – about four times[335]'. 'Doreen has, or had, two sons, one of whom I know died in Australia.'[336]*

The following marriages are based on information from Meriel Comerford and Jeremy Foster: Doreen married 1st in Kenya, to a serviceman named Jackie COOPER; 2nd to Michael (Mickey) MARRIOTT, by whom she had two sons:

> i) <u>Simon MARRIOTT</u> **^{3/1}** *'was killed in a car crash in America – leaving a wife and young son'[337]*:

> <u>Male MARRIOTT</u> **^{4/2}**

> ii) <u>Giles MARRIOTT</u> **^{3/1}** *'was killed in a freak motorbike accident on the Isle of Wight while holidaying there'[338]*.

She then had a relationship with a Bermudan millionaire, Reginald HOWARD-MAY (or HAYWARD-MAY), and then *'married a Baron VON KAGAR (spelling?) and lived in...a fashionable part of New York. On his death she moved to Spain (with a much younger man) whom she finally married'[339]*.

b. <u>Jasper Gilmore Herbert BELL</u> **²** (1923- ?), known as 'Gilmore', was born on 27 October 1923, and baptised at Chhindwara[340]:

> *'Baptisms solemnized at Chhindwara: 1924 April 30; born: 1923 October 27; Jasper Gilmore Herbert, son of Herbert Jasper and Eileen Gelston BELL; abode: Delhi; father's occ.: Executive Engineer, PWD; F.W. Martin, Chaplain of Nagpur'.*

He married Patricia FRENCH, divorced her, and they then re-married and lived on the S coast of England.

c. <u>Christopher Duncan BELL</u> **²** (1925- ?) was born on 8 July 1925 and baptised at Lahore in 1927[341]:

---

[334] OIOC (N/1/458/283).

[335] Meriel Comerford: e-mail (6.9.02).

[336] Meriel Comerford (App.A).

[337] Jeremy Foster: e-mail (10.9.02).

[338] ibid.

[339] Jeremy Foster: e-mail (10.9.02).

[340] OIOC (N/1/476/99).

[341] OIOC (N/1/498/148).

'Baptisms in the Archdeaconry of Lahore: 1927 Jany. 5th; born: 1925 July 8th; Christopher Duncan, son of Herbert Jasper and Eileen Gelston BELL; abode: New Delhi; father's occ.: Executive Engineer, PWD; T.H. Dixon, Chaplain of New Delhi'.

d. <u>Michael Dinwiddie BELL</u> [2] (1927- ?) was born on 6 October 1927, and his baptism is recorded in the General Register[342]:

'General register of baptisms: 1928 January 25; born: 1927 October 6; Michael Dinwiddie, male, parents: Herbert Jasper and Eileen Gelston BELL; abode: Akola[?]; father's occ.: Engineer, PWD; C.J. Ferguson Davie[?], Bishop, Acting Chaplain of Berar'.

"Michael died in South Africa, within the last 5 years, of heart and emphysema complications[343]'.

f. <u>Mary Frances Veronica BELL</u> [2] (1930- ?) was born on 8 June 1930, and her baptism is recorded in the General Register[344]:

'General register of baptisms: 1930 July 6th; born: 1930 June 8th; Mary Frances Veronica, daughter of Herbert Jasper and Eileen Gelston BELL; abode: Indore; father's occ.: PWD; G.W. Warmington, Chaplain of Mhow'.

She married Anthony GEORGE, known as 'Tony', Vice-Admiral, RN, ADC to HM the Queen, who is now retired. They live near Portsmouth. They had two daughters[345]:
   i) <u>Daughter GEORGE</u> [3/1]
   ii) <u>Daughter GEORGE</u> [3/1]

g. <u>David BELL</u> [2] (c.1932- ?) was the sixth child. I could not find his baptism record in the British Library (OIOC), and he may have been baptised in Kenya, or even born in Kenya. He married Julia ....and had (at least) two children:
   i) <u>Charles BELL</u> [3/1]
   ii) <u>Amy BELL</u> [3/1]

"David, who is a little older than Jeremy (I think) lives, as far as I know, in Perth, Western Australia. We met him and his then wife Julia (a charming girl) when the ship which was bringing us to Australia, the OLD Oriana! called in at Fremantle, which is more or less the port for Perth - they had no children at that stage, but eventually had Charles and Amy...'[346].

---

[342] OIOC (N/1/516/40).

[343] Jeremy Foster: e-mail (10.9.02).

[344] OIOC (N/1/534/131).

[345] Meriel Comerford (App.A).

[346] ibid.

3. <u>Norah Estelle GILMORE</u> [1/1] (1902-1959) was born on 30 June 1902, and baptised at Chhindwara[347]:

> *'Baptisms solemnized at Chhindwara, Church of England, C..P [Central Provinces]: 1902 August 31st; born: 1902 June 30th; Nora [sic] Estelle; Female; father: Walter Gelson and Mary Emily GILMORE; abode: Chhindwara; oc.: Forest Officer; S. Scott, Chaplain'.*

She came back from school in England with Eileen and Peggy in 1920 or 1921 as money was short and they had not seen their parents since 1914. The girls rejoined their parents at Raipur, where Walter GILMORE was in charge of the North Raipur Forest Division.

Norah married Esmond Lewis Pearce FOSTER on the 25 September 1926, from the house of her Aunt Mary GILMORE, somewhere in the New Forest. They honeymooned driving around Europe. Norah was refused entry to the Monte Carlo casino because they thought she was under age. Esmond had to go back to the hotel to fetch her passport. The couple won the amateur mixed foursomes at San Remo Golf Club, on the Italian Riviera, during their honeymoon. Granny FOSTER (Alma Douglas) cabled them during their honeymoon to say she was joining them with Aunt Madge, and drove over with Raisin, her chauffeur. Norah was not amused but Esmond managed to divert the ladies and continued with his honeymoon alone with his bride.

Esmond FOSTER was educated at public school and Oxford. In 1922 he moved to Seoni as an assistant Forest Officer, where he met the GILMORES. He was transferred to South Chanda Division, which he described as being hotter than the hinges of hell, but very beautiful. There he worked under Hugh GEORGE, who later became Conservator and finished his career as Chief Conservator of the Central Provinces. In 1926-1927 Esmond and Norah moved to Yeotmal after their honeymoon. They were in Melghat in 1928-1931. They lived in an old forest house, and Esmond described it as the happiest days of their lives..

In 1931-1935 they were stationed in Raipur, and in 1935-1942 Esmond was Chief Forest Officer, Andaman Islands, initially on Ross Island, Port Blair (1935) and then Haddo, Port Blair (1936-1942) (see his book for details of life in the Andamans). The decision was reached to evacuate after Singapore fell in 1942. Esmond escaped as the Japanese advance party arrived. He was awarded an OBE in 1942. In 1945 he took part in the re-occupation force, and I well remember seeing the Foster family embark on the Hooghly Docks in Calcutta, for their voyage back to the Andamans. Esmond and Norah did much to make good and repair the damage and horrors caused to the Islands and the people by the Japanese. Esmond retired in 1948. He wrote "Family Stories and Other Papers" from which much of the information in this family history is taken.

> Norah and Esmond moved from India to Northern Rhodesia after WW2, where Esmond worked for the Forestry Service before retiring at Fourways Farm, Miengwe, near Ndola, where I visited them in 1957, and where they are buried. They had four children:

---

[347] OIOC (N/1/301/157).

*Fosters and Duncans, Kharagpur, India (c.1939); left to right: Philippa DUNCAN,
Meriel FOSTER, Jill FOSTER, Felicity FOSTER, Brian DUNCAN.*

a. <u>Felicity Alma Mary Pearce FOSTER</u> [2] (b.1927) [shangrila@intekom.co.za] married
   John S. C. TENNENT, and had five children:

    i) <u>David Esmond TENNENT</u> [2/1]

    ii) <u>Jonathan George TENNENT</u> [2/1], known as 'Jonty' [baddog@mweb.co.za].

    iii) <u>Nicholas John TENNANT</u> [2/1] [ntennent@iafrica.com].

    iv) <u>Sarah Felicity TENNENT</u> [2/1]

    v) <u>Estelle TENNENT</u> [2/1]

b. <u>Norah Meriel Pearce FOSTER</u> [2] (b.1929), known as 'Meriel', 'Merry' or 'Mel', was
   born in Nagpur, India. She married Duane E. COMERFORD. They lived in
   Northern Rhodesia, now Zambia, and now live in Australia [61 Byrne Street,
   Lapstone, NSW 2773; merielc@bigpond.com.au], and had three children:

i) Timothy Duane COMERFORD [2/1] (b.1956)

ii) Norah Louise COMERFORD [2/1] (b.1959) known as 'Louise', *"has a degree in Early Childhood Development, and is teaching a class of troubled and low-mentality children. Her husband, Hugh, is a teacher, too, and teaches Science, Physics and maths in a High School"*[348]. They have two daughters, and live in Glenbrook, NSW:
> Lauren …… [3] (b.c.1986)
> Rebecca …… [3] (b.c.1988)

iii) Michael Esmond COMERFORD [2/1] (b.1965) [mcomerford@cdm.com.au] is a computer expert. He married Belinda …., and had three sons:
> Christopher COMERFORD [3] (b.c.1990)
> Alexander COMERFORD [3] (b.c.1994)
> Jeremy COMERFORD [3] (b.c.1999)

iv) Bruce COMERFORD [2/1] (b.1969) [pbruce1@optusnet.com.au] is a High School teacher, and lives in Glenbrook, NSW. He married Philippa ……, and had a daughter:

> Faith COMERFORD [3/2] (b.2001)

My daughter Caroline visited Meriel and her family when she was in Australia in about 1985.

c. Jennifer Gillian Pearce FOSTER [2] (b.1931), known as 'Jill', was born in Nagpur, India. She married Paul WHEELER (b.1928) [Little How, 1 Vicarage Close, Farnham, Surrey GU9 8EU; tel: 01252-725690]. Paul is a solicitor, and they had four children:

i) Christopher John Lewis WHEELER [2/1] (b.1952) [cw@wheelerslaw.co.uk] was born in Lusaka, Zambia. He a solicitor, and is the historian of the GILMORE-FOSTER family. He married Catherine Shan RUSSELL (b.1958) and they had three children:
> Matthew David Lewis WHEELER [2/2] (b.1983).
> Natasha Hannah WHEELER [2/2] (b.1986).
> Alexa Estelle WHEELER [2/2] (b.1990).

ii) Paul Gelston WHEELER [2/1] (b.1954), known as 'Pip' [PWhe639992@aol.com], was born at Ndola, Zambia. He married Susan WHITE (b.1952), and they have two children:
> Lewis WHEELER [2/2] (b.1983).
> Chloe WHEELER [2/2] (b.1985).

iii) Briony Estelle WHEELER [2/1] (b.1956) [1965 Omni Boulevard, Mount Pleasant, S. Carolina 29466, nr. Charleston; tel: 843-856-0865; brionyy@msn.com] married Jeremy YOUNG (b.1948) and had two children:

---

[348] Meriel Comerford (App.A).

William YOUNG [2/2] (b.1986).
Tristan YOUNG [2/2] (b.1989).

iv) Norah Margaret WHEELER [2/1] (b.1960) was born in Lymington. She married Alasdair Gordon Terry PEPPER (b.1960) and had four children:
Harriet PEPPER [2/2] (b.1985).
Nicholas PEPPER [2/2] (b.1986).
Jonathan PEPPER [2/2] (b.1989).
Anna PEPPER [2/2] (b.1991).

d. Jeremy Esmond Pearce FOSTER [2] (1936-2016) [Hurst Hill, 10 Hurst Close, Hook Heath, Woking, Surrey GU22 0DU; tel: 01483-768861. Jeremy married Gilda GRAY, and had a daughter:

i) Antonia Pearce FOSTER [2/1], a solicitor [Antonia.Foster@carter-ruck.com].

4. Kathleen GILMORE [1/1] (1903- ?) known as 'Peggy', was born on 18 November 1903, and baptised on 31 December 1903[349]:

> *'Baptisms solemnised at Kamptee & outstations; Church of England, C.P.[Central Provinces]; Kathleen Margaret, female, father: Walter Gelstone [sic] & Mary Emily GILMORE; abode: Bilaspur; occ.: Extra Assistant Conservator of Forests; Cyril Price, MA, Chaplain'.*

She married Vivian Terence CROLEY, known as 'Terence', at Asirgarh, in February 1929[350]. He was the son of Dr Croley, who worked as a medical officer for the Bengal Nagpur Railway, and retired to 'Cresta', Barnhorn Road, Bexhill, Sussex.

Terence and Peggy lived in the flat next to ours in Godfrey Mansions, Garden Reach, Calcutta in 1945/46. They looked after Norah GILMORE and family after their evacuation from the Andaman Islands, via Calcutta. Terence led the Force 136 expedition to the Andaman Islands during the Japanese occupation, on which my father **Richard DUNCAN** was 2 i/c. While the expedition was away, we shared a house with Peggy Croley in Inner Flower Road, Colombo, Ceylon.

Terence worked in India after Independence, and retired to 5 Grove Pastures, Lymington, Hampshire, where he was a member of the Royal Lymington Yacht Club. I visited Terence, my godfather, and Peggy several times, and sometimes met Jeremy and Gilda FOSTER there. Jeremy can add detail to the above.

Peggy and Terence had a son:

a. Oliver Terence Musgrave CROLEY [2] (1931-c.1948) was born at Adra, India, on 16 May 1931:

---

[349] OIOC (N/1/314/46).

[350] mentioned in Terence's account of his Force 136 Expedition to the Andaman Islands in 1944.

'Born 16 May 1931; Adra; Oliver Terence Musgrave CROLEY; Male; father: Vivian Terence; British Church of England; occ.: Asst. Traffic Superintendent, BNR [Bengal Nagpur Railway], mother: Kathleen Margaret CROLEY; British Christian'.

Oliver was killed in a motor-cycle accident shortly after his 21st birthday.

CROLEY family group (England?): in chairs: Mrs CROLEY, Dr CROLEY; seated on ground (left to rt.): Unknown, Terence CROLEY, Betty DUNCAN, unknown, Kathleen (Peggy) CROLEY.

5. <u>Walter Charles Gelston GILMORE</u> [1/1] (1908-1942), known as 'Charles', was born on 6 March 1908, and baptised on 18 June 1908 at Indore[351]:

'Baptisms solemnised at Indore, Church of England, Central India: 1908 June 18th; born: 1908 March 6th; Walter Charles Gelston, male; father: Walter Gelston and Mary Emily GILMORE; abode: Indore; occ.: Conservative [sic] of Forests; E.D. Wright, Chaplain'.

---

[351] OIOC (N/1/348/182).

He joined the 2nd Battalion, 14th Punjab Regiment in Hong Kong, where he was in business, at the outbreak of WW2. He died on 9 April 1942[352], some four months after the island fell to the Japanese on Christmas Day 1941. He was buried in Grave 1.A.68 in the Stanley Military Cemetery, Hong Kong, just beyond the town of Stanley in the southern part of Hong Kong island.

---

[352] Commonwealth War Graves Commission website.

APPENDIX F:. LETTER FROM MERIEL COMERFORD

1st September, 2002

Dear Brian,

Thank you so much for your letter - it was grand hearing from you again, and I was interested in all you have been finding out. Incidentally, we moved north along the east coast of Australia last year, in April, and now live in a "seaside" village called Lemon Tree Passage. We have had our eldest son, Timothy, living with us since his nine-year partnership with a lass in Melbourne broke up, and we love having him with us - he works in the Hospitality Industry, and loves anything to do with water - so do I! - and we are so close to it - and he loves sailing. You and Tess would be most welcome, anytime, though I think the best time of the year is now, coming into our spring. Jeremy always seems to come in high summer, when it is not as nice, and very hot, but I know it is a time when things in HIS garden are dormant, and he can leave it safely! He has been to see us three or four times, and we always love his visits. Felicity and her younger daughter, Estelle, visited us in Lapstone, and we had a wonderful time with the "do you remembers" and laughing hilariously over childhood memories, and I think Estelle (who is a peach of a girl) thought we were quite mad!

Reverting to the family tree, Doreen Bell IS the eldest of that clan, followed by Gilmore, Christopher, Michael, and David - each of them, with the exception of Mary, have been married at least twice, and as I am out of touch with them, I have very little idea of their family situations - Doreen has, or had, two sons, one of whom I know died in Australia. Mary has two daughters, and is married to Tony George, who ended up as an R.N Admiral. Doreen must be, now, about 81 - which is weird to think about because the last time I met her was in Cape Town when I was about 23, and she must have been about 31! 50 YEARS ago - half a century! David, who is a little older than Jeremy (I think) lives, as far as I know, in Perth, Western Australia. We met him and his then wife Julia (a charming girl) when the ship which was bringing us to Australia, the OLD Oriana! called in at Fremantle, which is more or less the prot for Perth - they had no children at that stage, but eventually had Charles and Amy - but that's as far as my knowledge goes. Michael was, probably still is, in South Africa.

In my own family, Tim was born in 1956, and Louise in 1959 - she has two daughters, Rebecca and Lauren, who are now 14 and 15-and-a-half. Louise went to University about eight years ago, and has a degree in Early Childhood Development, and is teaching a class of troubled and low-mentality children. Her husband, Hugh, is a teacher, too, and teaches Science, Physics and maths in a High School. After Louise we have Michael, born in 1965, who is married to Belinda, and they have three sons, Christopher, now twelve, Alexander who is eight, and Jeremy, who is a gorgeous three-year old with a will of iron! Michael is a computer whizz - and I honestly don't know exactly what he does, as computer-wise I am a dummy, and my family always say that I am Technologically Challenged if not totally Disabled! Our last, Bruce, is married to Philippa, and they have the wonderful small Faith, who is not quite a year old. Bruce, born in 1969, is also a High School Science teacher, and he, too, is very good with computers. They live almost opposite to Louise and her family in Glenbrook in the Lower Blue Mountains of NSW - five minutes away from where we lived in Lapstone, and the two families are very close and happy together.

One thing you might be interested to know is that the Fosters returned to the Andamans in three "lots" - first my Pappa, who went in on a "mercy ship" to relieve the suffering of the people there, who had been badly treated by the Japanese - the army was supposed to get there first and receive the surrender of the Japanese, but somehow, my father got there first, and was met on the jetty at Aberdeen by the little Japanese Admiral (afterwards executed for war crimes) who raced up to Daddy and handed over his sword - which Daddy as hastily handed back, and told the man he had better surrender to the army - they were coming along behind!   After Daddy, my Mamma went in to the Andamans with a section of the Red Cross (she had the rank of Major), and finally, when it was considered safe enough, we three girls and Jeremy went back to the Andamans - we had spent the time after we left school with Peggy and Terence in Nagpur (which is where I was born) and had a wonderful Christmas with them. Felicity was then about 18, and I was sixteen, and we helped with the Red Cross work of feeding and caring for the villagers, specially Felicity, who could drive and she was a very able lieutenant for Mummy, who wasn't well a lot of the time at that stage.   All four of us had been with our parents when the evacuation of the Andamans happened, and Mummy was in charge of all the women and children who were on the Maharajah - and we saw very little of her on that voyage, as she was busy with the women, most of whom hadn't been out of the Andamans for practically all their lives, and were terribly afraid.   We four weren't in the least concerned at the possible dangers we were facing, blacked out at night, and with heavy tarpaulins covering the sides of the ship all the time.   We each had an "emergency" pack which contained things like our topees, and a few necessities - I can't remember all of it, but I DO remember that Jeremy had his own tiny suitcase in which were HIS survival rations - his topee and a bar of chocolate!   We DID survive of course, without any incidents at all, but I think Mummy must have had a bad and worrying time with huge responsibilities, not only the safety of her own children.   We had wonderful parents.   Daddy later left the Andamans with the two Forest Department launches, the Jarawa and the Norah.   He was a very good seaman, and loved sailing and anything to do with the sea - and TREES! - but he didn't have very much, if any, navigational skills, but he managed to head for Madras, and reached, eventually, Vizagapatam, which is not far north of Madras, which was pretty good going, I think.   We four, but specially, I think, my sisters and I, had the most wonderful and fascinating childhoods - but as I have told Jeremy often, I think we are "dinosaurs" left over from a life and time which no longer exists and is, unbelievably, so long ago.   We four finally left the Andamans in 1946/47, before our parents finally did.   THEY left the Andamans and went to stay in Nyasaland (Malawi) with your grandparents, and Felicity, who wasn't happy in England, went to join them.   Incidentally, from Mummy I learned a phrase that your grandmother, Dulcie, used to use frequently - I think to urge on a donkey, and to this day, if I am urging on something or something, I say "Come, come, Tilly - come ON"! From there, because there was no work for Daddy in Nyasaland, they went to Ndola, where Daddy joined the Forest Department of Northern Rhodesia, and Jill and I flew out in 1948, to be followed at the end of his school year at Stubbington, by Jeremy.   Duane and I, seeing what was coming, left NR in late 1964, and came here - Duane to a new career, which he had to start from the very beginning (he was a Chief Inspector of Police in NR, and before that spent five years with the British army).   We came with two "African" children, and added two Australian ones - though we are all now, officially, Australians, and have never regretted for one moment our decision to come here - it is a wonderful country, and again, we have been marvelously lucky and very happy.

While we were in Ooty, and at Nazareth Convent, I went down with diphtheria, and was confined to one room - and only allowed visitors once I started to improve, and then Jill and Felicity used to come and visit me - standing OUTSIDE my bedroom window, and Felicity, never a great reader, used to stand patiently reading endlessly to me, as I could never get enough books - they had to be burnt after I had read them.   Why I'm telling you all this is that your mother, Aunty Betty to us, came and visited me in the same fashion - OUTSIDE the window! - and she asked if there was anything I would like, and I promptly answered yes, BOOKS - and shortly over, a parcel of books arrived and allayed my intense boredom for a little while.   No radio, or TV or even a phone line!   How DEPRIVED we were, weren't we?!   But how very lucky, too.

Reverting to my parents wedding - they were married in Ringwood, which IS in the New Forest, and they DID honeymoon in Europe - mostly, I think, in Italy, and I can remember Mummy telling me a story of going into an Italian shop to buy some elastic, and tried every way she knew, without words, but with hands and gestures, to describe what she needed, until it finally dawned on the shop-keeper and he said "Ah, ELASTICO"!   I think Mummy learned a lot about the Italian language then and there!   Add an O to any word!   Good fun.   They toured Europe - but I don't know which bits of it - much later, when they had all three of we girls, and they took with them our Ayah, who was with us for 18 years - and for the first time in Ayah's life she had to wear specially made warm underclothing and get a passport.   When she first saw snow she asked what all the "nimuc" (salt) was spread around for, and Mummy told her to pick some up and see what it tasted like - and Ayah was shocked to the core! That reminds me a little of when we were way out in the bush in NW NR, Duane and I, on the banks of the Zambesi, and the local Africans used to ask us what the sea was like - and we found it horrendously difficult to explain it, too, as they had no conception of any such thing.   We were fairly high above the Zambesi, and on the other side of the river were vast plains stretching out as far as you could see, with quite a lot of trees, but not very dense, and during the rainy season the whole of the plains flooded and looked like an endless lake with the trees standing feet deep in the water - we used to sit out in the garden to have our "chota pegs" in the evening and watch the sun going down, and the trees reflected in that huge expanse of water - and it was superb.   As I mentioned a wonderful childhood, so too, Duane and I have had a wonderful life and interesting, too.

I don't think I have any photographs which would be of much use to you - Jeremy has all the family photographs - and you might be interested in seeing the albums which Mummy and Daddy kept - huge, very heavy carved leather tomes!   I was delighted to see the one of Granny's wedding, which you provided - I hadn't even known there WAS one.   I'd have loved to have met her - Daddy always said that everyone adored her.   I DID meet WG, but I only remember him when he was more or less dying, and we went to Gelston House - not to stay IN the house - we had huge tents pitched in the grounds.   I remember being taken into his bedroom, where he was lying on a huge four-poster, against a pile of white pillows, and I remember him coming to the verandah rails outside his bedroom, and hawking and spitting over the rails!   His second wife, Lil, was a holy terror, and spent her time shouting at us, and I remember being thoroughly scared when she caught us running and chasing each other around the huge dining-room table!   I don't think Grandpa's daughters cared for her much, either, specially as after he died, she spirited away all the very few pathetic jewels Granny had owned.   NOT a nice woman, I think - and why on earth did he marry her?   Granny died of what was known, in those days, as "dropsy" - which was an accumulation of fluid in her body, and I think must have been due to high blood pressure - and could so easily be coped with nowadays.   She died in a rather nice way. Mummy, mine, was changing her bed, and WG picked Granny up his arms, and she started singing the Naughty Waltz - which I can still remember, and as she sang "Lift me lightly, hold me tightly, to that Naughty Waltz", she died.   I wish I had known her.

I've probably bored the socks off you, but hopefully, you have a "delete" button, and failing that - a WPB!

Thank you again for your letter - and please do keep up the good word and keep in contact with me - it's rather fun having an "extended" family, with all the "do you remembers"!

As ever,
Meriel, Merry, Mel!

APPENDIX G: THE SEARCH FOR MARY LEECH'S ANTECEDANTS

We know that Mary died on 22 August 1855; her burial record[353] states:

> '*2nd August 1855; Mary DUNCAN; 34 years; wife of George DUNCAN, Depty. Commissary of Ordnance, N.I. [Native Infantry] Force; buried 23rd August 1855; Ward Manle(?), Catechist'.*

So we can estimate that Mary was born in about 1820-1822, although the ecclesiastical records are not always accurate. I searched for the baptism record of a Mary LEECH born in 1820-23, but could not find it. She might have come out to India from Britain.

It's possible that Mary's mother was named 'Maria' or 'Eliza' because they are the names she gave her children by William PASLEY.

The following is a complete list of baptisms in Madras Presidency in 1808-1839:

It will be worth checking them for family names, and for possible mention of 'Mary', 'Checky' and 'Peece'

The difference in the spelling of the surnames – LEACH, LEECH, and LEITCH – is not very important, as there were often inconsistencies in spelling until the mid-1800s.

Surname	Christian names	Year of baptism	File ref. (N/2/ vol/folio)	Notes
LEECH	Nancy	1808	3/351	
LEECH	Joanah	1809	11/227	
LEECH	Sarah	1813	5/291	
LEACH	Mary Ann	1815	5/539	Too early, and 2nd name Ann does not appear elsewhere?
LEECH	John	1815	5/560	
LEECH	Neil	1816	6/223	
LEECH	Archibald	1819	7/69	
LEITCH	Mary	1822	8/294	Wrong surname and native mother
LEECH	Maria	1824	9/58	Dangerously ill when baptised, native mother
LEECH	Thomas	1824	9/81	
LEACH	Sophia	1827	23/103	
LEECH	George	1833	15/149	
LEACH	Joseph	1834	15/178	

---

[353] OIOC (N/2/35/92).

LEECH	Margaret	1836	16/159	
LEACH	Charles	1837	16/322	
LEACH	Eliz. Emily	1839	19/52	

A. Mary Anne LEACH (b.1814):

A possible baptism record for 'our' Mary LEECH is:

> '*Baptisms at Bangalore, 7 February 1815; This is to certify that Mary Anne, daughter of John LEACH, Corporal H.M. 32nd Dragoons, and .....born 17th October 1814, was baptised according to the form of public baptism set forth in the rubric of the Church of England this Seventh day of February 1815 by me (signed) W.Thomas, Chaplain; sponsors: William Clarke, Papa Blelcker, Checky Leach*'.

Militating against this being 'our' Mary is that:

a. The second name 'Anne' was never used in subsequent records, e.g. marriage and baptism of children;

b. This 'Mary Anne' would have been about 21 when she married William PASLEY in 1835 (her age not given in marriage record), and 26 when she married George Roan DUNCAN in 1840 (age not given in marriage record). However, when she died at Sitabuldi, Nagpur, in 1855, her age was given as 34 years, not 41 (which would have been the case if she was born in 1814). Nevertheless, there are many instances of inaccuracies in age in the ecclesiastical records.

B. Mary LEITCH (b.c.1822)

A Mary LEITCH is recorded[354] as baptised in 1822:

> '*Masulipatam: 29th October 1822; Mary, daughter of John LEITCH, Private in the M.E.[Madras European] Regt.doing duty at Masulipatam, and Patamaha a Native woman, was this day Baptised by me; R..W....., Chaplain.*'

Could this be the same person as John LEECH (below), probably not, since John LEECH was in HM's Army, whereas John LEITCH was in the HEIC Army (and in the same regiment as George Roan Duncan I). Nevertheless, the name of the native wife is the same.

The spelling of family names was very variable before about the mid-1850s, and no doubt LEITCH and LEECH were interchangeable. However, this 'Mary' would have been described as an 'Indo-Briton', not as a 'European'.

C. Mary LEECH (b.1819, Bengal)

A Mary LEECH was born in Meerut, Bengal, in 1819:

---

[354] OIOC (N/2/8/294).

'Meerut 1819: Mary; parents: Thomas LEECH & Mary; rank etc.: Private, 14th Regiment of Foot; born: 14th March'.

I doubt this was 'our' Mary, because there was not much movement of families between Presidencies, i.e. between Bengal and Madras in that period.

There seem to have been two LEECH/LEACH families in the Madras Presidency at the time:

a. <u>John LEECH</u> (? –1826?) was a private in HM 80th Regiment and/or HM 53rd Regiment. He had several children by an Indian woman named Pattamah:

Archibald LEECH baptised in 1819, son of John LEECH, Pvt. In HM 53rd Regiment, and Pattamah *'a native woman*[355]*'.*

Maria LEECH, born 5 January 1824, baptised in Masulipatam on 10 January 1824 *'being dangerously ill'*, daughter of the late John LEECH and Patamah, *'a native woman*[356]*'.*

I don't think our Mary LEECH can be from this parentage, because she is twice described as 'European' (in her marriage record, and the baptism record of her child). Not only was the name different, but Maria would have been just 11 years old at the time of marriage to William Pasley in April 1835. In any case, there's a strong probability that this Maria Leech died.

This was possibly the same John LEECH who had a son in 1816[357] although the regiment is different.

'Quilon; 4th November 1816; Neil, son of John and Fatima LEECH; H.M. 80th Regt.; born 3rd November 1816; was this day fully baptized by me (signed) Jas. Hutchison, Chaplain'.

b. <u>John LEECH</u>, a Warrant Officer (Conductor of Ordnance) in the Madras Army, who married Helen ZSCHERPEL (1803-aft.1822) in 1819. She was only 15 at the time of the marriage. The marriage record[358] states:

'St Mary's Church, Madras: 10th February 1819; John LEECH, Conductor of Ordnance of this Establishment, Bachelor; and Helen ZSCHERPEL, Spinster, were married in this Church St Mary's by licence of the Right Honorable The Governor, this day, by me, W.A. Heating, Chaplain; witnesses: Anthony French, John Heal'.

This John LEECH died intestate in 1822[359]:

'Funerals performed by laymen & Missionaries reported October to Snr. Chaplain Fort St George, 1822 Novr. 19th: John LEECH, Conductor [of Ordnance], Vipery[360], E.A.G. Falcke, Port Missionary'.

---

[355] OIOC (N/2/7/69).

[356] OIOC (N/2/9/58).

[357] OIOC (N/2/6/223).

[358] OIOC (N/2/7/109).

[359] OIOC (N/2/8/540).

[360] Vepery was a suburb of Madras.

The administration record of his estate[361] describes him as *'late Conductor of Ordnance'* and states: *'Helen LEECH of Madras, the widow of the said John LEECH, hath renounced the Right to the Administration of his Estate'.* There is no mention of a daughter, Mary.

However, if Mary was born in ca.1821, it would be in the feasible period of John LEECH's life, i.e. from his marriage in 1819 to his death in 1822.

Helen's family, the Zscherpels, lived in Madras at the time, descendants of Johan Friederich Zscherpel (c.1770-1819) and Christina, his wife. Johan is usually described as 'John Frederich' or 'Frederick', and was probably of German or Austrian origin. He and Christina had a child, John Frederick, probably an eldest son, in 1788[362]. He was baptised in St Mary's, Fort St George, so we know that the Zscherpels were in Madras from that year. In the baptisms of two of his children, he is described as 'Master of the Band of Musicians, 2nd Ba Euro Arty (and Coast Artillery).

Helen ZSCHERPEL, christened 'Helenna' was baptised on 5 November 1803:

> *'Duplicate register of Baptisms at St Mary's Parish, Fort St George: November 5th 1803: Helenna, daughter of Frederick ZSCHERPEL and Chistianna his wife'.*

No other likely candidates were baptised in India during the period. Nor could I find a baptism of anyone who might fit 'Peece LEECH', the witness at Mary's marriage in 1835.

Discussion

I'm not yet convinced that 'our' Mary LEECH came from the above families. It is more likely that a girl of 14-15 marrying in 1835 in Bangalore would have been born in India than have come out to India as a child. If Mary was born in India, why can't we find her baptism record? The OIOC ecclesiastical records are only about 80% complete. If Mary was born in Britain, it will be very difficult to trace her. She might have come to India as a maidservant, in which case there's a chance she might be listed in the HEIC Court Minutes.

It seems probable that Mary was an orphan when she was married in 1835, or at least without a father. We cannot know until we find out who 'Peece LEECH' was. Indeed, I must examine all the LEECH marriage and baptism records at OIOC.

Another avenue for research is the military records of LEECH men. These records do not always indicate children, but it should be possible to find the name of the ship in which the man came to India, and then find the passenger list.

The following LEECH candidates were found in the embarkation records:

> a. <u>John LEECH</u> attested to the HEIC as a labourer at Portsmouth, Hampshire, on 2 February 1818, aged 20, embarking on the *Phoenix* on 20 February 1818, landing at Madras. It's very doubtful that this man would have been a Conductor of Ordnance in 1819 (when John LEECH married Helen ZSCHERPEL), but he may be the John LEITCH in C. (above).

---

[361] OIOC (L/AG/34/29/222/ff.12&13).

[362] OIOC (N/2/2/56).

b. <u>John LEECH</u>[363] was a Bombadier, 1st(?) Battalion, Horse Artillery (Bengal or Madras?), from Sleigham(?), Yorkshire, came to India on the *Cambrian*, and died on 23 June 1842, intestate.

---

[363] OIOC (L/MIL/11/101).

APPENDIX H. DESCENDANTS OF ROBERT DUNCAN

I created this this Appendix in March 2017 after receiving additional information from Denise Taylor, a descendant of Robert Duncan. She contacted me while I was on holiday in SE Asia, and we later exchanged information.

Robert DUNCAN [2GGU] (after 1793- after 1866) was the eldest son of William and Rebecca Duncan (see Chapter 1). Robert married Anne WOODLOCK and had at least four children, born in Limerick[364]:

1. Rebecca DUNCAN [1/3] (1831- ?) married William LAWDLER on September 26, 1857[365].

2. George DUNCAN [1/3] (c.1834- ?). According to a letter written by his father (see App. A), he was *'a fine looking man, over 6 feet in height'*[366], and was *'serving in the police in Leeds'*[367] in 1866/67 (date of letter).

The family listed below is not confirmed yet, but there are some compelling connections that make me confident that they are 'our' Duncans. It's worth listing these connections:

- Thomasina, Robert, and George, are all family names, and the first rather unusual.

- George Duncan (son of Robert) was probably born in Ireland.

- We know from Robert Duncan's letter to his brother that his son George Duncan went to Leeds, and this family lived in Leeds, where the younger children (below) were born.

- George Duncan's wife (Nellie/Delia) was not only born in Ireland, but in Limerick, where Robert Duncan was living in the mid-1860s. Cindy Wood thinks that the names 'Nellie' and 'Delia' could easily have been confused in transcribing the census documents (Delia is a nickname for Bridget!).

According to Denise Taylor: George married Bridget Fitzgerald in Galway on February 5, 1853.

George was a Sub-Constable in the Royal Irish Constabulary; he served for about ten years from July 17, 1852 to November 25, 1862. He met his wife through her father, who was a colleague in the RIC. They had three children in Limerick before leaving for England, where he joined the Leeds Police on December 18, 1863. They then had another three children. George left the police on June 15, 1866 and then found work as a charge hand in iron works.[368]

The 1881 Census records, at 12 Briar St., Linthorpe[369] [Middlesborough], Yorks.: George DUNCAN, head, 51 (i.e. born in c.1830), born in Ireland; occupation: *'charging .... (iron)'*, and Nellie DUNCAN, wife, 48, born in Ireland, with the following children[370]:

---

[364] Denise Taylor, personal communication, March 2017

[365] Denise Taylor, personal communication, March 2017.

[366] Letter No 1 from Robert Duncan to George Roan Duncan I (6 July 1866/7).

[367] ibid.

[368] Denise Taylor, personal communication, March 2017

[369] 'Linthorpe' is not listed in my atlas, but there is a 'Linthorpe Road' in Middlesborough, running N-S through the center of the city.

[370] Denise Taylor, personal communication, March 2017

a. <u>Mary Ann DUNCAN</u> [2/2] (1859-aft.1875) born in Li.merick, married David POTTS on April 18, 1875[371]. They had a child:

    i) <u>Ada Isabella POTTS</u> [2/3] (1878-1959)\

b) <u>John DUNCAN</u> [2/2] (c.1861- ?) was recorded in the 1881 Census as aged 21, born in Ireland, and working as an engine driver. In the 1901 Census he is recorded as aged 40, born in Ireland, a boarder at 81 Christian Street, Liverpool, and working as an 'Engine Fitter'. He married Jane Groome in 1883; at the time he was living at 17 Briar St., Middlesborough[372].

c) <u>Thomasina DUNCAN</u> [2/2] (c.1864) was not recorded in the 1881 Census, probably because she would have left home (aged 17). She is recorded in the 1901 Census as a married woman (Thomasina HENDERSON), aged 37, born in Ireland. The census image is not clear about the age, but it's most probably 37 and not 34. Also, if she was born in about 1864 in Ireland, she fits neatly between elder brother John, and younger brother Robert. Moreover, her marriage record (below) shows that she was living at 17 Briar Street, near 12 Briar Street, where her father was living in 1881. The marriage record also shows her father's name as 'George'.

Thomasina was probably named after her aunt, <u>Thomasina DUNCAN</u> [1/3] (ca.1848-aft.1870) (see below). She married in Middlesborough on 2 October 1883[373], Tom HENDERSON, son of Robert Henderson:

> *'Marriage solemnised at the Parish Church of All Saints, Middlesborough, Yorkshire: Tom HENDERSON, 23, Bachelor, Clerk, 23 Suffield Street, father: Robert Henderson (Tailor); Thomasina DUNCAN, 20, Spinster, 17 Briar Street, father: George Duncan (Gas-man), in the presence of Robert DUNCAN and Emily Florence DUNCAN'.*

The witness 'Robert Duncan' might have been the bride's brother, or her grandfather. The other witness, 'Emily Florence', was Thomasina's younger sister (see below).

Thomasina and Tom Henderson were recorded in the 1901 Census[374], living at 3 Newport Road, Middlesborough, i.e. next door to her brother Robert (see below). Tom's occupation was 'Tobacco Dealer', working at home. They had the following children recorded in the 1901 Census:

Tomasina and Tom had two children:

    i) <u>Florence Hannah HENDERSON</u> [3/1] (1885- ?), who married Alexander Thomson (b.1834)[375]. According to the 1911 Census they were living at Craigmoor. Linden Grove, Middlesborough; he worked as a bank clerk (in Bradford).

---

[371] Denise Taylor, personal communication, March 2017

[372] Denise Taylor, personal comm.,, March 15, 2017

[373] GRO (MXB 506332).

[374] PRO ref: RG 13/4577.

[375] Denise Taylor, personal comm.,, March 15, 2017

ii) <u>Maud Wittington HENDERSON</u> [3/1] (1887- ?) who married, on June 3, 1915, Eric Christopher Lightfoot King (1888-1957)[376]. He served in the RASC in WW1 (#327026). They had a child:

<u>Alexander Christopher KING</u> [4] (1916-?), born on February 4, 1916 at Middlesborough.

d) <u>Robert Ely DUNCAN</u> [2/2] (c.1866-1902) was recorded in the 1881 Census as aged 16, born in Leeds, working as an errand boy. He is recorded in the 1901 Census[377] as 'Robert E. Duncan', aged 35, a Hotel (Pub) Manager, living (and working) at 1 Newport Road, Middlesborough, Yorkshire, i.e. next door to the Hendersons (above). There is a record of a Robert DUNCAN married Mary Ellen Duxbury[378]. (Also: a Robert DUNCAN married in Leeds District in Oct.-Dec.1890 (vol.9b, f.802). In the 1901 Census, Robert's wife is recorded as 'Mary E. Duncan', aged 31, born in Leeds, the pub manageress. Robert died, aged 37 on October 2, 1902; his wife died on September 16, 1935. Their gravestones, with their son George, are in plots D and P in Redcar Cemetery[379].

The following children are recorded in the 1901 Census:

i) <u>George Percival DUNCAN</u> [3/1] (1896-1918) born in Durham. He died aged 23, presumably unmarried.

ii) <u>Ivy DUNCAN</u> [3/1] (1899- ?), born in Middlesborough on November 1, 1899. She married James Edward McCue (1896-1974), and had two children:

<u>Peter McCUE</u> [4] (1922-2009) married Ruth Tombs, and had a son:

<u>Angus W, McCUE</u> [5].

<u>Donald J. McCUE</u> [4] (b.1927).

e) <u>Emily Florence DUNCAN</u> [2/2] (1867-aft.1881) aged 14 in the 1881 Census, born in Leeds. She was not recorded in the 1901 Census, probably because she had married. She married Samuel Alfred Lees, a solicitor's clerk, in 1889[380]. They had two children:

i) <u>Duncan Griffiths LEES</u> [3/1] (1894-1966) who was born in Middlesborough, and married Margaret Elizabeth Grunwell in Middlesborough. They had a child:

<u>Ivy LEES</u> [4] (1924- ?) born in Middlesborough.

ii) <u>Evelyn M. LEES</u> [3/1] (1900- ?)

---

[376] Ibid.

[377] PRO ref: RG 13/4577.

[378] Denise Taylor, personal comm.. March 2017. GRO, June 1891 (9d, 780).

[379] Ibid

[380] Denise Taylor, personal comm.. March 2017.

f) <u>George William DUNCAN</u> [2/2] (c.1870- ?) aged 11 in the 1881 Census, born in Middlesborough on May 16, 1869[381]. He married Mary Emily Cockburn[382]. Note that a 'George William Duncan' was married in Middlesborough in the March Quarter of 1895 (9d, 604 or 694), when he would have been about 25 years old. George was recorded in the 1901 Census[383] living at 15 High Street, Stockton, Co. Durham, where he had a tobacconist business (his brother-in-law, Tom Henderson – see above – was a tobacco dealer). Living with him were his wife, 'Mary E. DUNCAN', aged 32, born in Houghton Le Spring, County Durham, and three children, and a servant.

George married (1895) Mary Emily Cockburn (1867-1959) and had three children:

i) <u>Hilda Mary DUNCAN</u> [2/2] (1896-aft.1901), the grandmother of my correspondent Denise Tayor, was born in Stockton in the December 1895 quarter[384]. She married (January 26, 1919) Roydon Williard James Macleod. She served in France in WW1; he was a driver in the RASC. They had six children:

> <u>Robert Duncan Roydon MACLEOD</u> [3/1] (1920- ?)
>
> <u>Duncan MACLEOD</u> [3/1] (1923- ?)
>
> <u>Bensley Follit MACLEOD</u> [3/1] (1924-)
>
> <u>Joyce MACLEOD</u> [3/1] (1926-)
>
> <u>Sheila Jean MACLEOD</u> [3/1] (1933-2016)
>
> <u>Mary MACLEOD</u> [3/1] (died aged 16)

ii) <u>George Victor DUNCAN</u> [2/2] (1898-aft.1901), known as 'Victor', was born in Stockton in the June 1897 quarter[385]. He married Bessie Kidd, and they had two children:

> <u>Peter M. DUNCAN</u> [3/1] (b.1937) in Cleveland, Yorkshire.
>
> <u>Robert Anthony DUNCAN</u> [3/1] (1945-2016) in Durham, known as Tony. He married Jane (nee ?) and had two children:
>
>> <u>Paul DUNCAN</u> [4]
>>
>> <u>Peter DUNCAN</u> [4]

iii) <u>Ada DUNCAN</u> [2/2] (1899- ?) was born in Stockton in the June 1899 quarter[386]. She married Albert Atkinson, and had no children. He was a foreman loco fitter, and they lived at 4 Marske Mill Terrace, Redcar, near Saltburn, Yorkshire[387].

---

[381] Ibid.

[382] Ibid.

[383] PRO: RG13/4626/141/28/168.

[384] 1901 Census & Free BMDs, Dec. 1895, Stockton (10a, 84).

[385] 1901 Census & Free BMDs, June 1897, Stockton (10a, 82).

[386] 1901 Census & Free BMDs, June 1899, Stockton (10a, 49).

[387] Denise Taylor, personal comm.., March 2017.